William James Linton

Rare Poems of the 16th and 17th Centuries

William James Linton

Rare Poems of the 16th and 17th Centuries

ISBN/EAN: 9783337006105

Printed in Europe, USA, Canada, Australia, Japan

Cover: Foto ©Thomas Meinert / pixelio.de

More available books at **www.hansebooks.com**

RARE POEMS

OF THE

SIXTEENTH AND SEVENTEENTH CENTURIES

A SUPPLEMENT TO THE ANTHOLOGIES

COLLECTED AND EDITED WITH NOTES
BY W. J. LINTON

LONDON: KEGAN PAUL, TRENCH, & CO

MDCCCLXXXIII

The engraving on the Title-page borrowed
from a design by the great Scottish painter

DAVID SCOTT

SECOND EDITION.

UNDER the title GOLDEN APPLES OF HESPERUS I lately printed a limited edition (only 225 copies) of " Poems not in the Collections," meaning the general selections accessible to the ordinary readers — not really students of English poetry. The present book is but in part a reprint of that. Half the wood-cuts omitted, some new ones are given; and instead of poems of the 19th century, additional poems of the 16th and 17th centuries, with a selection from the anonymous writings of the same period, out of early miscellanies, or from reprints by Park, Ellis, Collier, Arber, &c. The Notes are all new.

Some very few of these contents of my book may possibly be found in one or other anthology, escaping my search; half a dozen in Ward's *English Poets*, 1880 (obtained after I had arranged my work), I have thought it worth while to retain, for reasons stated in my Notes. Of the Anonymous Poems, one or two, now and then accidentally appearing in some out of the way collection, I have repeated for the sake of nearer completeness of this division of my subject. My book here meets a want, whether to be accounted for by the insufficient industry of collectors, or for other reasons, I need not care to determine. It is enough to state the fact, while redeeming so much of neglected worth as may be within reach of one who claims not scholarship, but dares to call himself a lover of the old writers.

Toward a correct text I have done all an unlearned man is able to do, taking for guide the belief that our poets were not writers of nonsense.   My book meant for the general reader, old spelling is preserved only in those few places in which the modernizing would disturb either the measure or the rhyme: e.g. — (pp. 1–2) *herbis, stalkis, thingis; mene* for moan, and (p. 6) *hert* for heart.   For old spelling else, beyond antiquarian interest, I have no more respect than for printers' points. There were no established rules in those days : authors were lawless ; careless or uncertain even as to their proper names. "Our ancestors, finding it absolutely impossible to adopt any consistent mode of orthography, fairly left it to the discretion or caprice of the several writers and transcribers." (ELLIS — *Introductory Remarks on Language*.)   There is applicable truth too in the confession of the printer of Sidney's *Arcadia*, that "being spred abroade in written coppies" (note here the spelling revised !) *much corruption had been gathered by ill writers*. For punctuation, since Arber, Ellis, Collier (it may be closely following the copy before them), to say nothing of editors not so accomplished, do, sometimes, play havoc with their author's meaning, I have ventured to judge for myself : and to punctuate according to context and the obvious or the seeming intention of the writer.   All important changes will be acknowledged in the Notes.   I ask the more learned student's mercy where I go wrong.

New-Haven, Conn., U. S. A.
1882.

CONTENTS

PART II—AUTHORS UNKNOWN

PART I—KNOWN AUTHORS

INHERITORS OF UNFULFILL'D RENOWN

SHELLEY

POEMS

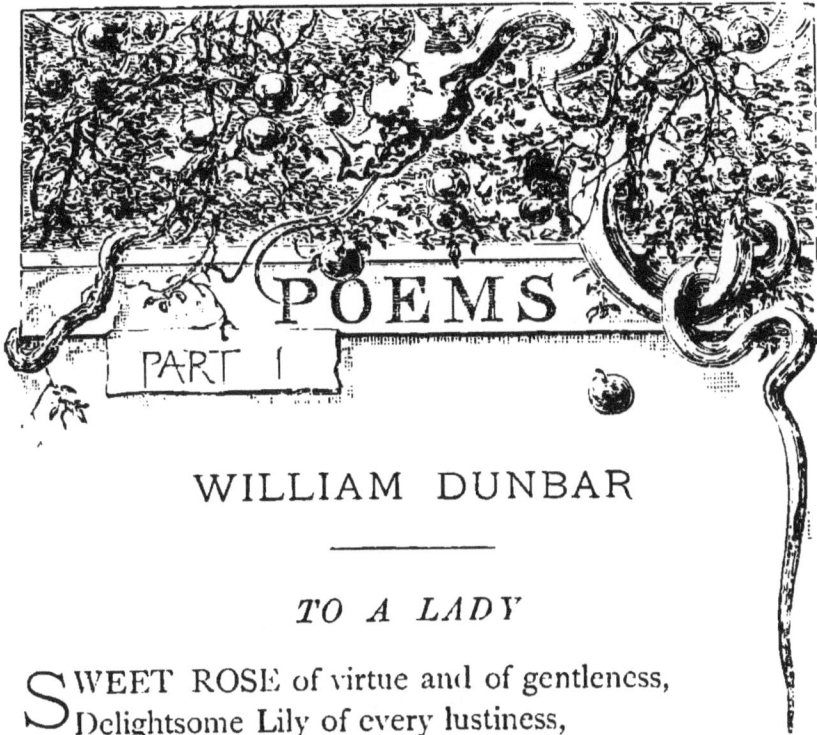

WILLIAM DUNBAR

TO A LADY

SWEET ROSE of virtue and of gentleness,
Delightsome Lily of every lustiness,
   Richest in bounty and in beauty clear
   And every virtue that to heaven is dear,
   Except only that ye are merciless!

Into your garth this day I did pursue:
There saw I flowers that fresh were of hue,
   Both white and red most lusty were to seen,
   And wholesome herbis upon stalkis green;
   Yet leaf nor flower find could I none of Rue.

I doubt that March, with his cold blastis keen,
Has slain this gentle herb that I of mene:
   Whose piteous death does to my heart such pain
   That I would make to plant his root again,
   So comforting his leaves unto me been.

ADVICE TO LOVERS

IF ye would love and lovèd be,
In mind keep well these thingis three,
And sadly in thy breast imprent, —
    Be secret, true, and pâtient !

For he that patience can not leir,
He shall displeasance have perquier,
Though he had all this worldis rent :
    Be secret, true, and patiènt !

For who that secret can not be,
Him all good fellowship shall flee,
And credence none shall him be lent :
    Be secret, true, and patiènt !

And he that is of heart untrue,
From he be ken'd, farewell ! adieu !
Fie on him ! fie ! his fame is went :
    Be secret, true, and patiènt !

Thus he that wants ane of these three
Ane lover glad may never be,
But aye in some thing discontent :
    Be secret, true, and patiènt !

Nought with thy tongue thyself discure
The thingis thou hast of nature ;
For if thou dost, thou should repent :
    Be secret, true, and patiènt !

JOHN HEYWOOD

A PRAISE OF HIS LADY

GIVE PLACE, you Ladies ! and begone ;
   Boast not yourselves at all !
For here at hand approacheth One
   Whose face will stain you all.

The virtue of her lively looks
   Excels the precious stone ;
I wish to have none other books
   To read or look upon.

In each of her two crystal eyes
   Smileth a naked boy :
It would you all in heart suffice
   To see that lamp of joy.

I think Nature hath lost the mould
   Where She her shape did take ;
Or else I doubt if Nature could
   So fair a creature make.

She may be very well compared
   Unto the Phœnix kind,
Whose like was never seen or heard
   That any man can find.

In life she is Diana chaste,
   In truth Penelope ;
In word and eke in deed steadfast :
   What will you more we say ?

If all the world were sought so far,
   Who could find such a wight?
Her beauty twinkleth like a star
   Within the frosty night.

Her rosiall colour comes and goes
   With such a comely grace,
More readier too than doth the rose,
   Within her lively face.

At Bacchus' feast none shall her meet,
   Ne at no wanton play,
Nor gazing in an open street,
   Nor gadding as a stray.

The modest mirth that she doth use
   Is mix'd with shamefacedness ;
All vice she doth wholly refuse,
   And hateth idleness.

O Lord ! it is a world to see
   How virtue can repair
And deck in her such honesty
   Whom Nature made so fair.

Truly She doth as far exceed
   Our women now-a-days
As doth the gillyflower a weed,
   And more a thousand ways.

How might I do to get a graff
   Of this unspotted tree?
For all the rest are plain but chaff
   Which seem good corn to be.

This gift alone I shall her give :
    When Death doth what he can,
Her honest fame shall ever live
    Within the mouth of man.

SIR THOMAS WYATT

YEA OR NAY

MADAM ! Withouten many words, —
    Once I am sure you will, or no :
And if you will, then leave your boordes
    And use your wit and show it so !

For with a beck you shall me call ;
    And if of One that burns alway
Ye have pitie or ruth at all,
    Answer him fair with Yea or Nay !

If it be Yea, I shall be fain ;
    If it be Nay, friends as before,
You shall another man obtain,
    And I, mine own, be yours no more.

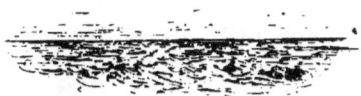

DISDAIN ME NOT!

The Lover prayeth not to be disdained, refused, mistrusted, nor forsaken.

DISDAIN me not without desert !
  Nor leave me not so suddenly !
Since well ye wot that in my hert
  I mean ye not but honestly.

Refuse me not without cause why !
  Forethink me not, to be unjust !
Since that by lot of fantasy
  This careful knot needs knit I must.

Mistrust me not ! though some there be
  That fain would spot my steadfastness.
Believe them not ! since that ye see
  The proof is not as they express.

Forsake me not till I deserve !
  Nor hate me not till I offend !
Destroy me not till that I swerve,
  But since ye know what I intend !

Disdain me not that am your own !
  Refuse me not that am so true !
Mistrust me not till all be known !
  Forsake me not, ne for no new !

THOMAS, LORD VAUX

DEATH IN LIFE

HOW can the tree but waste and wither away
That hath not sometime comfort of the sun?
And can the flower but fade and soon decay
   That always is with dark clouds overrun?
Is this a life?   Nay! death I may it call,
That feels each pain and knows no joy at all.

What foodless beast can live long in good plight?
   Or is it life where senses there be none?
Or what availeth eyes without their sight?
   Or else a tongue to him that is alone?
Is this a life?   Nay! death I may it call,
That feels each pain and knows no joy at all.

Whereto serve ears if that there be no sound?
   Or such a head where no device doth grow
But all of plaints, since sorrow is the ground
   Whereby the heart doth pine in deadly woe?
Is this a life?   Nay! death I may it call,
That feels each pain and knows no joy at all.

THOMAS TUSSER

SOME pleasures take
    And can not give,
But only make
    Poor thanks their gift;
Some, meaning well,
    In debt do live,
And can not tell
    Where else to shift.

Some knock, and fain
    Would ope the door,
To learn the vain
    Good turn to praise;
Some shew poor face,
    And be but poor,
Yet have a grace
    Good fame to raise.

Some owe and give
    Yet still in debt,
And so must live,
    For aught I know;
Some wish to pay,
    And can not get,
But night and day
    Must still more owe.

Even so must I, for service past,
Still wish you good while life doth last.

NICOLAS GRIMAÒLD

A TRUE LOVE

WHAT sweet relief the showers to thirsty plants we see,
What dear delight the blooms to bees, my true Love is to me :
As fresh and lusty Ver foul Winter doth exceed,
As morning bright with scarlet sky doth pass the evening's weed,
As mellow pears above harsh crabs esteemed be,
So doth my Love surmount them all whom yet I hap to see.
The oak shall olives bear, the lamb the lion fray,
The owl shall match the nightingale in tuning of her lay,
Or I my Love let slip out of mine entire heart :
So deep reposèd in my breast is She for her desert.
For many blessed gifts, O happy, happy land !
Where Mars and Pallas strive to make their glory most to stand ;
Yet, land ! more is thy bliss that in this cruel age
A Venus imp thou hast brought forth, so steadfast and so sage.
Among the Muses nine a tenth if Jove would make,
And to the Graces three a fourth, Her would Apollo take.
Let some for honour hunt, or hoard the massy gold :
With Her so I may live and die, my weal can not be told.

BARNABE GOOGE

TO THE TUNE OF APELLES

THE rushing rivers that do run,
  The vallies sweet adorned new
That lean their sides against the sun,
  With flowers fresh of sundry hue,
Both ash and elm, and oak so high,
Do all lament my woeful cry.

While winter black with hideous storms
  Doth spoil the ground of summer's green,
While spring-time sweet the leaf returns
  That late on tree could not be seen,
While summer burns, while harvest reigns,
Still, still do rage my restless pains.

No end I find in all my smart,
  But endless torment I sustain,
Since first, alas ! my woeful heart
  By sight of thee was forced to plain, —
Since that I lost my liberty,
Since that thou madest a slave of me.

My heart, that once abroad was free,
  Thy beauty hath in durance brought ;
Once reason ruled and guided me,
  And now is wit consumed with thought ;
Once I rejoiced above the sky,
  And now for thee, alas ! I die.

Once I rejoiced in company,
    And now my chief and sole delight
Is from my friends away to fly
    And keep alone my wearied sprite.
Thy face divine and my desire
From flesh have me transform'd to fire.

O Nature ! thou that first didst frame
    My Lady's hair of purest gold,
Her face of crystal to the same,
    Her lips of precious rubies' mould,
Her neck of alabaster white, —
Surmounting far each other wight :

Why didst thou not that time devise,
    Why didst thou not foresee, before
The mischief that thereof doth rise
    And grief on grief doth heap with store,
To make her heart of wax alone
And not of flint and marble stone?

O Lady ! show thy favour yet :
    Let not thy servant die for thee !
Where Rigour ruled let Mercy sit !
    Let Pity conquer Cruelty !
Let not Disdain, a fiend of hell,
Possess the place where Grace should dwell !

ONCE MUSING AS I SAT,
  And candle burning by,
When all were hush'd, I might discern
  A simple sely Fly,
That flew before mine eyes,
  With free rejoicing heart,
And here and there with wings did play,
  As void of pain and smart.
Sometime by me she sat
  When she had play'd her fill ;
And ever when she rested had
  About she flutter'd still.
When I perceived her well
  Rejoicing in her place,
O happy Fly ! quoth I, and eke
  O worm in happy case !
Which of us two is best?
  I that have reason? No:
But thou that reason art without,
  And therewith void of woe.
I live, and so dost thou ;
  But I live all in pain,
And subject am to Her, alas !
  That makes my grief her gain.
Thou livest, but feel'st no grief;
  No love doth thee torment.
A happy thing for me it were
  (If God were so content)
That thou with pen wert placèd here
  And I sat in thy place :
Then I should joy as thou dost now,
  And thou shouldst wail thy case.

SIR PHILIP SIDNEY

THE MEETING

IN A GROVE, most rich of shade,
Where birds wanton music made,
May, then young, his pied weeds showing,
New-perfumed with flowers fresh growing,

Astrophel with Stella sweet
Did for mutual comfort meet,
Both within themselves oppressed,
But each in the other blessed.

Him great harms had taught much care,
Her fair neck a foul yoke bare ;
But her sight his cares did banish,
In his sight her yoke did vanish.

Wept they had, alas the while !
But now tears themselves did smile,
While their eyes, by love directed,
Interchangeably reflected.

Sigh they did : but now betwixt
Sighs of woe were glad sighs mix'd ;
With arms cross'd, yet testifying
Restless rest, and living dying.

Their ears hungry of each word
Which the dear tongue would afford,
But their tongues restrain'd from walking
Till their hearts had ended talking.

But, when their tongues could not speak,
Love itself did silence break ;
Love did set his lips asunder,
Thus to speak in love and wonder.

Stella ! sovereign of my joy,
Fair triumpher of annoy !
Stella, star of heavenly fire !
Stella, loadstar of desire !

Stella, in whose shining eyes
Are the lights of Cupid's skies,
Whose beams, where they once are darted,
Love therewith is straight imparted !

Stella, whose voice, when it speaks,
Senses all asunder breaks !
Stella, whose voice, when it singeth,
Angels to acquaintance bringeth !

Stella, in whose body is
Writ each character of bliss ;
Whose face all all beauty passeth,
Save thy mind, which yet surpasseth !

Grant, O grant, —— but speech, alas !
Fails me, fearing on to pass ;
Grant, — O me ! what am I saying?
But no fault there is in praying :

Grant — O Dear ! on knees I pray,
(Knees on ground he then did stay),
That, not I, but since I love you,
Time and place for me may move you.

Never season was more fit ;
Never room more apt for it ;
Smiling air allows my reason ;
These birds sing — " Now use the season ! "

This small wind, which so sweet is,
See how it the leaves doth kiss !
Each tree in its best attiring,
Sense of love to love inspiring.

Love makes earth the water drink ;
Love to earth makes water sink ;
And, if dumb things be so witty,
Shall a heavenly grace want pity ?

There his hands, in their speech, fain
Would have made tongue's language plain ;
But her hands, his hands repelling,
Gave repulse all grace excelling.

Then she spake : her speech was such
As not ears but heart did touch ;
While such wise she love denièd
As yet love she signifièd.

Astrophel ! said she, — my love
Cease in these effects to prove !
Now be still ! yet still believe me,
Thy grief more than death would grieve me.

If that any thought in me
Can taste comfort but of thee,
Let me, fed with hellish anguish,
Joyless, hopeless, endless languish !

If those eyes you praisèd be
Half so dear as you to me,
Let me home return stark-blinded
Of those eyes, and blinder-minded !

If to secret of my heart
I do any wish impart
Where thou art not foremost placèd,
Be both wish and I defacèd !

If more may be said, I say :
All my bliss in thee I lay :
If thou love, my love content thee !
For all love, all faith is meant thee.

Trust me, while I thee deny,
In myself the smart I try ;
Tyrant Honour doth thus use thee ;
Stella's self might not refuse thee.

Therefore, Dear ! this no more move,
Lest, though I leave not thy love,
Which too deep in me is framèd,
I should blush when thou art namèd ! —

Therewithal away she went,
Leaving him so passion-rent
With what she had done and spoken,
That therewith my song is broken.

ABSENCE

O DEAR LIFE ! when shall it be
That mine eyes thine eyes shall see,
  And in them thy mind discover :
Whether absence have had force
Thy remembrance to divorce
  From the image of thy lover?

O, if I myself find not
After parting aught forgot
  Nor debarr'd from Beauty's treasure,
Let not tongue aspire to tell
In what high joys I shall dwell !
  Only thought aims at the pleasure.

Thought ! therefore I will send thee
To take up the place for me ;
  Long I will not after tarry :
There, unseen, thou may'st be bold
Those fair wonders to behold
  Which in them my hopes do carry.

Thought ! see thou no place forbear !
Enter bravely everywhere !
  Seize on all to her belonging !
But if thou wouldst guarded be,
Her beams fearing, take with thee
  Strength of liking, rage of longing !

Think of that most grateful time,
When my leaping heart will climb
  In my lips to have his biding :

There those roses for to kiss,
Which do breathe a sugar'd bliss,
   Opening rubies, pearls dividing !

Think of my most princely power,
Which, I blessed, shall devour
   With my greedy licorous senses
Beauty, music, sweetness, love,
While she doth against me prove
   Her strong darts but weak defences !

Think, think of those dallyings
When, with dove-like murmurings,
   With glad moaning, passed anguish,
We change eyes and, heart for heart,
Each to other do depart
   Joying till joy makes us languish !

O, my Thought ! thy thoughts surcease !
Thy delights my woes increase ;
   My life melts with too much thinking :
Think no more, — but die in me
Till thou shalt revivèd be,
   At her lips my nectar drinking !

OPPORTUNITY

ONLY JOY ! now here you are,
Fit to hear and ease my care,
Let my whispering voice obtain
Sweet reward for sharpest pain :
Take me to thee, and thee to me ! —
" No, no, no, no, my Dear ! let be !"

Night hath closed all in her cloak ;
Twinkling stars love-thoughts provoke ;
Danger hence good care doth keep ;
Jealousy himself doth sleep :
Take me to thee, and thee to me ! —
" No, no, no, no, my Dear ! let be !"

Better place no wit can find,
Cupid's knot to loose or bind ;
These sweet flowers, our fine bed, too
Us in their best language woo :
Take me to thee, and thee to me ; —
" No, no, no, no, my Dear ! let be !"

This small light the moon bestows
Serves thy beams but to disclose,
So to raise my hap more high ;
Fear not, else none can us spy :
Take me to thee, and thee to me ! —
" No, no, no, no, my Dear ! let be !"

That you heard was but a mouse ;
Dumb sleep holdeth all the house ;
Yet asleep, methinks they say —
Young fools ! take time while you may :
Take me to thee, and thee to me ! —
" No, no, no, no, my Dear ! let be !"

Niggard Time threats, if we miss
This large offer of our bliss,
Long stay ere he grant the same :
Sweet ! then, while each thing doth frame,
Take me to thee, and thee to me ! —

"No, no, no, no, my Dear! let be!"

Your fair mother is a-bed,
Candles out and curtains spread;
She thinks you do letters write;
Write, but let me first indite:
Take me to thee, and thee to me!—
"No, no, no, no, my Dear! let be!"

Sweet! alas! why strive you thus?
Concord better fitteth us;
Leave to Mars the force of hands;
Your power in your beauty stands:
Take thee to me, and me to thee!—
"No, no, no, no, my Dear! let be!"

Woe to me, and do you swear
Me to hate but I forbear?
Cursèd be my destines all,
That brought me so high to fall!
Soon with my death I will please thee——
"No, no, no, no, my Dear! let be!"

THE COLLOQUY

"WHO is it that this dark night
Underneath my window plaineth?"—
It is one who, from thy sight
Being, ah! exiled, disdaineth
Every other vulgar light.

"Why, alas! and are you he?

Be not yet those fancies changèd?"—
    Dear! when you find change in me,
    Though from me you be estrangèd,
    Let my change to ruin be?

"Well, in absence this will die:
Leave to see, and leave to wonder!"—
    Absence sure will help if I
    Can learn how myself to sunder
    From what in my heart doth lie.

"But time will these thoughts remove:
Time doth work what no man knoweth."—
    Time doth as the subject prove:
    With time still affection groweth
    In the faithful turtle dove.

"What if we new beauties see?
Will not they stir new affection?"—
    I will think they pictures be,
    (Image-like of saints' perfection)
    Poorly counterfeiting thee.

"But your reason's purer light
Bids you leave such minds to nourish."—
    Dear! do reason no such spite:
    Never doth thy beauty flourish
    More than in my reason's sight.

"But the wrongs love bears will make
Love at length leave undertaking."—
    No! the more fools it do shake
    In a ground of so firm making,
    Deeper still they drive the stake.

" Peace ! I think that some give ear ;
Come no more, lest I get anger !" —
    Bliss ! I will my bliss forbear,
    Fearing, Sweet ! you to endanger ;
    But my soul shall harbour there.

" Well, begone ! begone ! I say :
Lest that Argus eyes perceive you." —
    O, unjust is Fortune's sway
    Which can make me thus to leave you,
    And from louts to run away.

EPITHALAMIUM

LET Mother Earth now deck herself in flowers,
   To see her offspring seek a good increase,
Where justest love doth vanquish Cupid's powers,
And war of thoughts is swallow'd up in peace,
    Which never may decrease,
    But, like the turtles fair,
  Live one in two, a well-united pair :
    Which that no chance may stain,
  O Hymen ! long their coupled joys maintain !

O Heaven ! awake, show forth thy stately face ;
Let not these slumbering clouds thy beauties hide,
But with thy cheerful presence help to grace
The honest Bridegroom and the bashful Bride,
    Whose loves may ever bide,
    Like to the elm and vine,
  With mutual embracements them to twine :

In which delightful pain,
O Hymen ! long their coupled joys maintain !

Ye Muses all ! which chaste affects allow
And have to Thyrsis shown your secret skill,
To this chaste love your sacred favours bow ;
And so to him and her your gifts distill
    That they all vice may kill
    And, like to lilies pure,
May please all eyes, and spotless may endure :
    Where that all bliss may reign,
  O Hymen ! long their coupled joys maintain !

Ye Nymphs which in the waters empire have !
Since Thyrsis' music oft doth yield you praise,
Grant to the thing which we for Thyrsis crave :
Let one time — but long first — close up their days,
    One grave their bodies seize ;
    And, like two rivers sweet
When they though divers do together meet,
    One stream both streams contain !
  O Hymen ! long their coupled joys maintain !

Pan ! father Pan, the god of silly sheep !
Whose care is cause that they in number grow, —
Have much more care of them that them do keep,
Since from these good the others' good doth flow ;
    And make their issue show
    In number like the herd
Of younglings which thyself with love hast rear'd,
    Or like the drops of rain !
  O Hymen ! long their coupled joys maintain !

Virtue, if not a God, yet God's chief part !
Be thou the knot of this their open vow :
That still he be her head, she be his heart ;
He lean to her, she unto him do bow ;
    Each other still allow ;
    Like oak and misletoe,
Her strength from him, his praise from her do grow !
    In which most lovely train,
  O Hymen ! long their coupled joys maintain !

But thou, foul Cupid, sire to lawless lust !
Be thou far hence with thy empoison'd dart,
Which, though of glittering gold, shall here take rust,
Where simple love, which chasteness doth impart,
    Avoids thy hurtful art,
    Not needing charming skill
Such minds with sweet affections for to fill :
    Which being pure and plain,
  O Hymen ! long their coupled joys maintain !

All churlish words, shrewd answers, crabbed looks,
All privateness, self-seeking, inward spite,
All waywardness which nothing kindly brooks,
All strife for toys and claiming master's right,
    Be hence aye put to flight ;
    All stirring husband's hate
'Gainst neighbours good for womanish debate
    Be fled : as things most vain !
  O Hymen ! long their coupled joys maintain !

All peacock pride and fruits of peacock's pride,
Longing to be with loss of substance gay,

With recklessness what may the house betide
So that you may on higher slippers stay,
  For ever hence away !
  Yet let not sluttery,
 The sink of filth, be counted housewifery,
  But keeping whole your main !
 O Hymen ! long their coupled joys maintain !

But above all, away vile jealousy,
The evil of evils, just cause to be unjust !
How can he love, suspecting treachery ?
How can she love, where love can not win trust ?
  Go, snake ! hide thee in dust ;
  Nor dare once show thy face
 Where open hearts do hold so constant place
  That they thy sting restrain !
 O Hymen ! long their coupled joys maintain !

The Earth is deck'd with flowers, the Heavens display'd.
Muses grant gifts, Nymphs long and joined life,
Pan store of babes, virtue their thoughts well stay'd,
Cupid's lust gone, and gone is bitter strife.
  Happy man ! happy wife !
  No pride shall them oppress,
 Nor yet shall yield to loathsome sluttishness ;
  And jealousy is slain,
 For Hymen will their coupled joys maintain.

WOOING STUFF

FAINT AMORIST! what, dost thou think
To taste Love's honey, and not drink
One dram of gall? or to devour
A world of sweet, and taste no sour?
Dost thou ever think to enter
Th' Elysian Fields, that darest not venture
In Charon's barge? A lover's mind
Must use to sail with every wind.
He that loves and fears to try
Learns his Mistress to deny.
Doth she chide thee? 'tis to show it
That thy coldness makes her do it;
Is she silent? is she mute?
Silence fully grants thy suit;
Doth she pout and leave the room?
Then she goes to bid thee come;
Is she sick? why then, be sure
She invites thee to the cure;
Doth she cross thy suit with No?
Tush! she loves to hear thee woo;
Doth she call the faith of man
In question? nay! she loves thee than;
And if e'er she makes a blot,
She's lost if that thou hitt'st her not.
He that after ten denials
Dares attempt no farther trials,
Hath no warrant to acquire
The dainties of his chaste desire.

RURAL POESY

O WORDS, which fall like summer dew on me !
  O breath, more sweet than is the growing bean !
O tongue, in which all honey'd liquors be !
O voice, that doth the thrush in shrillness stain !
   Do you say still this is her promise due :
   That she is mine, as I to her am true !

Gay hair, more gay than straw when harvest lies !
Lips, red and plump as cherries' ruddy side !
Eyes, fair and great, like fair great ox's eyes !
O breast, in which two white sheep swell in pride !
   Join you with me to seal this promise due :
   That she be mine, as I to her am true !

But thou, white skin, as white as curds well press'd,
So smooth as sleek-stone like it smoothes each part !
And thou, dear flesh, as soft as wool new dress'd,
And yet as hard as brawn made hard by art !
   First four but say, next four their saying seal ;
   But you must pay the gage of promised weal.

AN EPITAPH

H IS BEING was in her alone :
  And he not being, she was none.
They joy'd one joy, one grief they grieved ;
One love they loved, one life they lived.
The hand was one, one was the sword,
That did his death, her death afford.
As all the rest, so now the stone
That tombs the two is justly one.

STELLA ! the fullness of my thoughts of thee
  Can not be stay'd within my panting breast ;
But they do swell and struggle forth of me
Till that in words thy figure be express'd :
And yet, as soon as they so formed be,
According to my lord Love's own behest,
With sad eyes I their weak proportion see
To portrait that which in this world is best.
So that I can not choose but write my mind,
And can not choose but put out what I write :
While these poor babes their death in birth do find.
And now my pen these lines had dashed quite,
But that they stopp'd his fury from the same
Because their fore-front bare sweet Stella's name.

ALAS ! have I not pain enough, my friend !
  Upon whose breast a fiercer grip doth tire
Than did on him who first stole down the fire,
While Love on me doth all his quiver spend,
But with your rhubarb words you must contend
To grieve me worse, in saying that Desire
Doth plunge my well-form'd soul even in the mire
Of sinful thoughts which do in ruin end?
If that be sin which doth the manners frame,
Well-staid with truth in word and faith of deed,
Ready of wit, and fearing nought but shame, —
If that be sin which in fix'd hearts doth breed
A loathing of all loose unchastity, —
Then love is sin, and let me sinful be !

MY MUSE may well grudge at my heavenly joy
If still I force her in sad rhymes to creep :
She oft hath drunk my tears now hopes to enjoy
Nectar of mirth, since I Jove's cup do keep.
Sonnets be not bound 'prentice to annoy ;
Trebles sing high, so well as bases deep.
Grief but Love's winter livery is : the boy
Hath cheeks to smile, so well as eyes to weep.
Come then, my Muse ! show thou height of delight
In well-raised notes ; my pen, the best it may,
Shall paint out joy though but in black and white.
Cease, eager Muse ! peace, pen ! for my sake stay !
I give you here my hand for truth of this :
Wise silence is best music unto bliss.

MY TRUE LOVE hath my heart, and I have his,
By just exchange one for the other given :
I hold his dear, and mine he can not miss ;
There never was a bargain better driven.
His heart in me keeps me and him in one ;
My heart in him his thoughts and senses guides :
He loves my heart for once it was his own ;
I cherish his because in me it bides.
His heart his wound receivèd from my sight ;
My heart was wounded with his wounded heart :
For as from me on him his hurt did light,
So still methought in me his hurt did smart.
Both equal hurt, in this change sought our bliss :
My true love hath my heart, and I have his.

SIR EDWARD DYER

THE FRIEND'S REMONSTRANCE

PROMETHEUS, when first from heaven high
  He brought down fire, ere then on earth not seen,
Fond of delight, a Satyr, standing by,
Gave it a kiss, as it like sweet had been.
Feeling forthwith the other burning power,
Wood with the smart, with shouts and shrieking shrill,
He sought his ease in river, field, and bower ;
But for the time his grief went with him still.
So silly I, with that unwonted sight,
In human shape an angel from above,
Feeding mine eyes, the impression there did light ;
That since I run and rest as pleaseth Love.
The difference is : the Satyr's lips — my heart,—
He for a while, I evermore have smart.

HIS ANSWER

A SATYR once did run away for dread
  With sound of horn which he himself did blow :
Fearing and fear'd, thus from himself he fled,
Deeming strange ill in that he did not know.
Such causeless fears when coward minds do take,
It makes them fly that which they fain would have :
As this poor beast, who did his rest forsake,
Thinking not why but how himself to save.

Even thus might I, for doubts which I conceive
Of mine own words, my own good hap betray ;
And thus might I, for fear of may-be, leave
The sweet pursuit of my desirèd prey.
Better like I thy Satyr, dearest Dyer !
Who burn'd his lips to kiss fair shining fire.

Philip Sidney.

THOMAS WATSON

ON SIDNEY'S DEATH

HOW LONG with vain complaining,
With dreary tears and joys refraining,
    Shall we renew his dying
    Whose happy soul is flying,
    Not in a place of sadness,
    But in eternal gladness?
Sweet Sidney lives in heaven : then let our weeping
Be turn'd to hymns and songs of pleasant keeping !

OF TIME

TIME wasteth years and months and days and hours :
Time doth consume fame, honour, wit, and strength :
Time kills the greenest herbs and sweetest flowers :
Time wears out youth and beauty's looks at length :
Time doth convey to ground both foe and friend,
And each thing else but Love, which hath no end.

Time maketh every tree to die and rot :
Time turneth oft our pleasures into pain :
Time causeth wars and wrongs to be forgot :
Time clears the sky which first hung full of rain :
Time makes an end of all humane desire,
But only this which sets my heart on fire.

Time turneth into nought each princely state :
Time brings a flood from new resolvèd snow :
Time calms the sea where tempest was of late :
Time eats whate'er the moon can see below :
And yet no time prevails in my behove,
Nor any time can make me cease to love.

JEALOUS OF GANYMEDE

THIS latter night, amidst my troubled rest,
A dismal dream my fearful heart appall'd,
Whereof the sum was this : Love made a feast,
To which all neighbour Saints and Gods were call'd :
The cheer was more than mortal men can think,
And mirth grew on by taking in their drink.

Then Jove amidst his cups, for service done,
'Gan thus to jest with Ganymede, his boy :
I fain would find for thee, my pretty Son !
A fairer wife than Paris brought to Troy.
Why, Sir ! quoth he, if Phœbus stand my friend,
Who knows the world, this gear will soon have end.

Then Jove replied that Phœbus should not choose
But do his best to find the fairest face ;
And she once found should ne will nor refuse,
But yield herself and change her dwelling-place,

Alas ! how much was then my heart affright :
Which bade me wake and watch my Fair Delight.

THE KISS

IN time long past, when in Diana's chase
A bramble bush prick'd Venus in the foot,
Old Æsculapius help'd her heavy case
Before the hurt had taken any root :
Wherehence, although his beard were crisping hard.
She yielded him a kiss for his reward.

My luck was like to his, this other day,
When She whom I on earth do worship most
For kissing me vouchsafèd thus to say —
" Take this for once, and make thereof no boast !"
Forthwith my heart gave signs of joy by skips,
As though our souls had join'd by joining lips.

And since that time I thought it not amiss
To judge which were the best of all these three :
Her breath, her speech, or that her dainty kiss :
And (sure) of all the kiss best likèd me.
For that was it which did revive my heart,
Oppress'd and almost dead with daily smart.

PHILOMELA

WHEN May is in his prime and youthful Spring
Doth clothe the tree with leaves and ground
                    with flowers,
And time of year reviveth every thing.
And lovely Nature smiles, and nothing lours,
Then Philomela most doth strain her breast
With night complaints, and sits in little rest.

This bird's estate I may compare with mine,
To whom fond love doth work such wrongs by day
That in the night my heart must needs repine,
And storm with sighs to ease me as I may:
Whilst others are becalm'd, or lie them still,
Or sail secure with tide and wind at will.

And as all those which hear this bird complain
Conceive on all her tunes a sweet delight,
Without remorse or pitying her pain,
So She for whom I wail both day and night
Doth sport herself in hearing my complaint:
A just reward for serving such a Saint.

MY LOVE IS PAST

LOVE hath delight in sweet delicious fare;
Love never takes good Counsel for his friend;
Love author is and cause of idle care;
Love is distraught of wit and hath no end;
Love shooteth shafts of burning hot desire;
Love burneth more than either flame or fire.

Love doth much harm through jealousy's assault;
Love once embraced will hardly part again;
Love thinks in breach of faith there is no fault;
Love makes a sport of others' deadly pain;
Love is a wanton child, and loves to brawl;
Love with his war brings many souls to thrall.

These are the smallest faults that lurk in Love;
These are the hurts which I have cause to curse;
These are those truths which no man can disprove;
These are such harms as none can suffer worse.

All this I write that others may beware,
Though now myself twice free from all such care.

THE MAY-QUEEN

WITH fragrant flowers we strew the May,
   And make this our chief holy-day :
For though this clime were blest of yore,
Yet was it never proud before.
   O beauteous Queen of second Troy !
   Accept of our unfeigned joy !

Now th' air is sweeter than sweet balm,
And satyrs dance about the palm ;
Now earth, with verdure newly dight,
Gives perfect signs of her delight.
   O beauteous Queen of second Troy !
   Accept of our unfeigned joy !

Now birds record new harmony,
And trees do whistle melody ;
Now every thing that Nature breeds
Doth clad itself in pleasant weeds.
   O beauteous Queen of second Troy !
   Accept of our unfeigned joy !

SONNET

BLAME me not, dear Love ! though I talk at randon,
   Terming thee scornful, proud, unkind, disdainful,
Since all I do can not my woes abandon,
Or rid me of the yoke I feel so painful.
If I do paint thy pride or want of pity,
Consider likewise how I blaze thy beauty :

Inforcèd to the first in mournful ditty,
Constrained to the last by servile duty.
And take thou no offence if I misdeemed !
Thy beauty's glory quencheth thy pride's blemish :
Better it is of all to be esteemed
Fair and too proud than not fair and too squeamish.
And seeing thou must scorn, and 'tis approvèd,
Scorn to be ruthless since thou art belovèd !

ANTHONY MUNDAY

DIRGE FOR ROBIN HOOD

WEEP, weep, ye woodmen ! wail ;
   Your hands with sorrow wring !
Your master. Robin Hood, lies dead :
   Therefore sigh as you sing !

Here lie his primer and his beads —
   His bent bow and his arrows keen ;
His good sword and his holy cross :
   Now cast on flowers fresh and green !

And, as they fall, shed tears and say
   Well, well-a-day ! well, well-a-day !
Thus cast ye flowers fresh, and sing,
   And on to Wakefield take your way !

GEORGE PEELE

CUPID'S CURSE

Ænone — FAIR and fair and twice so fair,
    As fair as any may be,—
    The fairest shepherd on our green,
    A Love for any Ladie !
Paris — Fair and fair and twice so fair,
    As fair as any may be,—
    Thy Love is fair for thee alone,
    And for no other Ladie.
Ænone — My Love is fair, my Love is gay,
    As fresh as been the flowers in May ;
    And of my Love my roundelay,
    My merry merry merry roundelay,
      Concludes with Cupid's Curse —
    They that do change old love for new,
    Pray Gods, they change for worse !
Both — They that do change ——

Ænone — Fair and fair and twice so fair,
    As fair as any may be,—
    The fairest shepherd on our green,
    A Love for any Ladie !
Paris — Fair and fair and twice so fair,
    As fair as any may be,—
    Thy Love is fair for thee alone,
    And for no other Ladie.

ÆNONE — My Love can pipe, my Love can sing,
         My Love can many a pretty thing ;
         And of his lovely praises ring
         My merry merry roundelays :
             Amen to Cupid's Curse !
         They that do change old love for new,
             Pray Gods, they change for worse !
PARIS — They that do change old love for new,
             Pray Gods, they change for worse !
BOTH — Fair and fair ——

COLIN'S SONG

O GENTLE LOVE ! ungentle for thy deed,
         Thou makest my heart
         A bloody mark,
With piercing shot to bleed :
Shoot soft, sweet Love ! for fear thou shoot amiss,
         For fear too keen
         Thy arrows been
And hit the heart where my Belovèd is !

Too fair that fortune were, nor never I
         Shall be so blest
         Among the rest,
That Love shall seize on her by sympathy :
Then since with Love my prayèrs bear no boot,
         This doth remain
         To cease my pain :
I take the wound and die at Venus' foot.

ROBERT GREENE

DORON AND CARMELA

AN ECLOGUE

DORON

SIT DOWN, CARMELA! here are cobs for kings,
Sloes black as jet, or like my Christmas shoes;
Sweet cider, which my leathern bottle brings:
Sit down, Carmela! let me kiss thy toes!

CARMELA

Ah, Doron! ah, my heart! thou art as white
As is my mother's calf or brinded cow;
Thine eyes are like the slow-worm's in the night;
Thine hairs resemble thickest of the snow.

The lines within thy face are deep and clear,
Like to the furrows of my father's wain;
The sweat upon thy face doth oft appear,
Like to my mother's fat and kitchen gain.

Ah, leave my toes, and kiss my lips, my Love!
My lips are thine, for I have given them thee.
Within thy cap 'tis thou shalt wear my glove;
At foot-ball sport thou shalt my champion be.

DORON

Carmela dear ! even as the golden ball
That Venus got, such are thy goodly eyes ;
When cherries' juice is jumbled therewithal,
Thy breath is like the steam of apple pies.

Thy lips resemble two cucumbers fair ;
Thy teeth like to the tusks of fattest swine ;
Thy speech is like the thunder in the air :
Would God thy toes, thy lips, and all were mine !

CARMELA

Doron ! what thing doth move this wishing grief?

DORON

'Tis Love, Carmela ! ah, 'tis cruel Love
That, like a slave and caitiff villain thief,
Hath cut my throat of joy for thy behove.

CARMELA

Where was he born?

DORON

      I' faith I know not where :
But I have heard much talking of his dart.
Ay me, poor man ! with many a trampling tear,
I feel him wound the fore-horse of my heart.

What, do I love ?   O no, I do but talk ;
What, shall I die for love ?   O no, not so ;
What, am I dead ?   O no, my tongue doth walk :
Come kiss, Carmela ! and confound my woe !

CARMELA

Even with this kiss, as once my father did,
I seal the sweet indentures of delight :
Before I break my vow the Gods forbid !
No, not by day, nor yet by darksome night.

DORON

Even with this garland made of hollyhocks
I cross thy brows from every shepherd's kiss.
Heigh-ho, how glad am I to touch thy locks !
My frolic heart even now a freeman is.

CARMELA

I thank you, Doron ! and will think on you ;
I love you, Doron ! and will wink on you ;
I seal your charter-patent with my thumbs.
Come kiss, and part ! for fear my mother comes.

INFIDA'S SONG

SWEET ADON ! darest not glance thine eye —
     N'oserez-vous? mon bel ami !—
  Upon thy Venus that must die?
     Je vous en priè, pity me !
  N'oserez-vous? mon bel ! mon bel !
     N'oserez-vous? mon bel ami !

See how sad thy Venus lies,—
     N'oserez-vous? mon bel ami !—
  Love in heart and tears in eyes :
     Je vous en priè, pity me !
  N'oserez-vous? mon bel ! mon bel !
     N'oserez-vous? mon bel ami !

Thy face is fair as Paphos' brooks —
  N'oserez-vous? mon bel ami ! —
Wherein Fancy baits her hooks :
  Je vous en priè, pity me !
N'oserez-vous? mon bel ! mon bel !
  N'oserez-vous? mon bel ami !

Thy cheeks like cherries that do grow —
  N'oserez-vous? mon bel ami ! —
Amongst the western mounts of snow :
  Je vous en priè, pity me !
N'oserez-vous? mon bel ! mon bel !
  N'oserez-vous? mon bel ami !

Thy lips vermilion full of love,—
  N'oserez-vous? mon bel ami ! —
Thy neck as silver-white as dove :
  Je vous en priè, pity me !
N'oserez-vous? mon bel ! mon bel !
  N'oserez-vous? mon bel ami !

Thine eyes like flames of holy fires —
  N'oserez-vous? mon bel ami ! —
Burn all my thoughts with sweet desires :
  Je vous en priè, pity me !
N'oserez-vous? mon bel ! mon bel !
  N'oserez-vous? mon bel ami !

All thy beauties sting my heart ; —
  N'oserez-vous? mon bel ami ! —
I must die through Cupid's dart :
  Je vous en priè, pity me !
N'oserez-vous? mon bel ! mon bel !
  N'oserez-vous? mon bel ami !

Wilt thou let thy Venus die? —
    N'oserez-vous? mon bel ami! —
Adon were unkind, say I —
    Je vous en priè, pity me!
N'oserez-vous? mon bel! mon bel!
    N'oserez-vous? mon bel ami! —

To let fair Venus die for woe —
    N'oserez-vous? mon bel ami! —
That doth love sweet Adon so.
    Je vous en priè, pity me!
N'oserez-vous? mon bel! mon bel!
    N'oserez-vous? mon bel ami!

MENAPHON'S ROUNDELAY

WHEN tender ewes, brought home with evening sun,
    Wend to their folds,
    And to their holds
The shepherds trudge when light of day is done,
    Upon a tree
The Eagle, Jove's fair bird, did perch;
    There resteth he:
A little Fly his harbour then did search,
And did presume, though others laugh'd thereat,
To perch whereas the princely Eagle sat.

The Eagle frown'd, and shook his royal wings,
    And charged the Fly
    From thence to hie:
Afraid, in haste the little creature flings;
    Yet seeks again,

Fearful, to perk him by the Eagle's side :
   With moody vein
The speedy post of Ganymede replied —
Vassal ! avaunt ! or with my wings you die ;
Is 't fit an Eagle seat him with a Fly ?

The Fly craved pity ; still the Eagle frown'd :
   The silly Fly,
   Ready to die,
Disgraced, displaced, fell groveling to the ground :
   The Eagle saw,
And with a royal mind said to the Fly —
   Be not in awe !
I scorn by me the meanest creature die :
Then seat thee here ! The joyful Fly up flings,
And sate safe, shadow'd with the Eagle's wings.

SWEET CONTENT

SWEET are the thoughts that savour of content ;
 The quiet mind is richer than a crown ;
Sweet are the nights in careless slumber spent ;
The poor estate scorns Fortune's angry frown :
Such sweet content, such minds, such sleep, such bliss,
 Beggars enjoy, when princes oft do miss.

The homely house that harbours quiet rest,
The cottage that affords no pride nor care,
The mean agrees with country music best,
The sweet consort of mirth and modest fare,—
Obscurèd life sets down as type of bliss :
A mind content both crown and kingdom is.

MENAPHON'S SONG

SOME say — Love,
    Foolish Love,
Doth rule and govern all the Gods :
    I say — Love,
    Inconstant Love,
Sets men's senses far at odds.
    Some swear — Love,
    Smooth-faced Love,
Is sweetest sweet that man can have :
    I say — Love,
    Sour Love,
Makes Virtue yield as Beauty's slave :
A bitter sweet ; a folly worst of all,
That forceth Wisdom to be Folly's thrall.

    Love is sweet :
    Wherein sweet?
In fading pleasures that do pain?
    Beauty sweet :
    Is that sweet
That yieldeth sorrow for a gain?
    If Love 's sweet,
    Herein sweet —
That minutes' joys are monthly woes :
    'Tis not sweet
    That is sweet
Nowhere but where repentance grows.
Then love who list ! if beauty be so sour,
Labour for me ! love rest in prince's bower !

MICHAEL DRAYTON

WHAT LOVE IS

WHAT IS LOVE but the desire
　　Of that thing the fancy pleaseth?
A holy and resistless fire
　　Weak and strong alike that seizeth:
Which not Heaven hath power to let,
　　Nor wise Nature can not smother;
Whereby Phœbus doth beget
　　On the Universal Mother:
That the everlasting chain
　　Which together all things tied,
And unmoved doth them retain,
　　And by which they shall abide:
That consent we clearly find
　　Which doth things together draw
And so, strong in every kind,
　　Subjects them to Nature's law:
Whose high virtue Number teaches,
　　In which every thing doth move,
From the lowest depth that reaches
　　To the height of heaven above:
Harmony that, wisely found
　　When the cunning hand doth strike,
Whereas every amorous sound
　　Sweetly marries with the like.

The tender cattle scarcely take
From their dams, the fields to prove,
But each seeketh out a make :
Nothing lives that doth not love.
Not so much as but the plant —
As Nature every thing doth pair —
By it if the male do want,
Doth dislike and will not bear.
Nothing, then, is like to Love,
In the which all creatures be :
From it ne'er let me remove !
Nor let it remove from me !

ROWLAND'S ROUNDELAY

— To whom Her Swain, unworthy though he were,
Thus unto Her his Roundelay applies :
To whom the rest the under-part did bear.
Casting upon Her their still longing eyes.

Rowland — Of her pure eyes, that now is seen.
  Chorus — Come, let us sing, ye faithful swains !
Rowland — O She alone the Shepherds' Queen,
  Chorus — Her flock that leads :
      The Goddess of these meads,
      These mountains, and these plains.

Rowland — Those eyes of hers that are more clear
  Chorus — Than can poor shepherd's song express.
Rowland — Than be his beams that rules the year :
  Chorus — Fie on that praise
      In striving things to raise
      That doth but make them less !

Rowland — That do the flowery Spring prolong,
Chorus — So all things in her sight do joy,
Rowland — And keep the plenteous Summer young,
Chorus — And do assuage
The wrathful Winter's rage
That would our flocks annoy.

Rowland — Jove saw her breast that naked lay,
Chorus — A sight most fit for Jove to see,
Rowland — And swore it was the Milky Way:
Chorus — Of all most pure
The path, we us assure,
To his bright court to be.

Rowland — He saw her tresses hanging down,
Chorus — That movèd with the gentle air,
Rowland — And said that Ariadne's Crown
Chorus — With those compared
The Gods should not regard,
Nor Berenice's Hair.

Rowland — When She hath watch'd my flocks by night,
Chorus — O happy flocks that She did keep!
Rowland — They never needed Cynthia's light,
Chorus — That soon gave place,
Amazèd with her grace
That did attend thy sheep.

Rowland — Above, where heaven's high glories are,
Chorus — When She is placèd in the skies,
Rowland — She shall be call'd the Shepherds' Star:
Chorus — And evermore
We shepherds will adore
Her setting and her rise.

SONG OF MOTTO AND PERKIN

MOTTO — Tell me, thou skilful shepherd swain !
　　　　Who's yonder in the valley set?
PERKIN — O, it is She whose sweets do stain
　　　　The lily, rose, the violet.

MOTTO — Why doth the Sun, against his kind,
　　　　Stay his bright chariot in the skies?
PERKIN — He pauseth, almost stricken blind
　　　　With gazing on her heavenly eyes.

MOTTO — Why do thy flocks forbear their food,
　　　　Which sometime was their chief delight?
PERKIN — Because they need no other good
　　　　That live in presence of her sight.

MOTTO — How come these flowers to flourish still,
　　　　Not withering with sharp Winter's death?
PERKIN — She hath robb'd Nature of her skill,
　　　　And comforts all things with her breath.

MOTTO — Why slide these brooks so slow away,
　　　　As swift as the wild roe that were?
PERKIN — O muse not, shepherd ! that they stay.
　　　　When they her heavenly voice do hear.

MOTTO — From whence come all these goodly swains
　　　　And lovely girls attired in green?
PERKIN — From gathering garlands on the plains,
　　　　To crown thy Syl : our shepherds' Queen.

The sun that lights this world below,
Flocks, brooks, and flowers, can witness bear,
These shepherds and these nymphs do know,
Thy Sylvia is as chaste as fair.

TO HIS COY LOVE

I PRAY THEE leave, love me no more,
   Call home the heart you gave me :
I but in vain that Saint adore
   That can, but will not save me.
These poor half-kisses kill me quite ;
   Was ever man thus servèd,
Amidst an ocean of delight
   For pleasure to be stervèd?

Show me no more those snowy breasts,
   With azure riverets branched,
Where, whilst mine eye with plenty feasts,
   Yet is my thirst not staunched.
O Tantalus ! thy pains ne'er tell,—
   By me thou art prevented :
'Tis nothing to be plagued in hell,
   But thus in heaven tormented !

Clip me no more in those dear arms,
   Nor thy life's comfort call me !
O these are but too powerful charms,
   And do but more enthrall me.
But see how patient I am grown
   In all this coil about thee !
Come, Nice Thing ! let thy heart alone,
   I can not live without thee.

JOHN DAVIES

OF HEREFORD

THE PICTURE OF AN HAPPY MAN

HOW BLESS'D is he, though ever cross'd,
That can all crosses blessings make ;
That finds himself ere he be lost,
And lose that found, for virtue's sake.

Yea, bless'd is he in life and death,
That fears not death, nor loves this life ;
That sets his will his wit beneath ;
And hath continual peace in strife.

That striveth but with frail Desire,
Desiring nothing that is ill ;
That rules his soul by Reason's squire,
And works by Wisdom's compass still.

That nought observes but what preserves
His mind and body from offence ;
That neither courts nor seasons serves,
And learns without experience.

That hath a name as free from blot
As Virtue's brow, or as his life
Is from the least suspect or spot,
Although he lives without a wife.

That doth, in spite of all debate,
    Possess his soul in patience ;
And pray, in love, for all that hate ;
    And hate but what doth give offence.

Whose soul is like a sea too still,
    That rests, though moved : yea, moved (at least)
With love and hate of good and ill,
    To waft the mind the more to rest.

That singly doth and doubles not;
    But is the same he seems ; and is
Still simply so, and yet no sot,
    But yet not knowing ought amiss.

That never sin concealed keeps.
    But shows the same to God, or moe ;
Then ever for it sighs and weeps.
    And joys in soul for grieving so.

That by himself doth others mete,
    And of himself still meekly deems ;
That never sate in scorner's seat ;
    But as himself the worst esteems.

That loves his body for his soul,
    Soul for his mind, his mind for God,
God for Himself ; and doth controul
    CONTENT, if it with Him be odd.

That to his soul his sense subdues,
    His soul to reason, and reason to faith ;
That vice in virtue's shape eschews,
    And both by wisdom rightly weigh'th.

That rests in action, acting nought
   But what is good in deed and show ;
That seeks but God within his thought,
   And thinks but God to love and know.

That, all unseen, sees all (like Him),
   And makes good use of what he sees ;
That notes the tracks and tricks of Time,
   And flees with the one, the other flees.

That lives too low for envy's looks,
   And yet too high for loath'd contempt ;
That makes his friends good men and books,
   And nought without them doth attempt.

That lives as dying, living yet
   In death, for life he hath in hope ;
As far from state as sin and debt,
   Of happy life the means and scope.

That fears no frowns, nor cares for fawns
   Of Fortune's favourites, or foes ;
That neither checks with kings nor pawns,
   And yet still wins what checkers lose.

That ever lives a light to all,
   Though oft obscurèd, like the sun ;
And though his fortunes be but small,
   Yet Fortune doth not seek, nor shun.

That never looks but grace to find,
   Nor seeks for knowledge to be known ;
That makes a kingdom of his mind,
   Wherein, with God, he reigns alone.

This man is great with little state,
   Lord of the world epitomized :
Who with staid front out-faceth Fate ;
   And, being empty, is sufficed,—
Or is sufficed with little, since (at least)
He makes his conscience a continual feast.

IN PRAISE OF MUSIC

THE motion which the nine-fold sacred quire
   Of angels make : the bliss of all the bless'd,
Which (next the Highest) most fills the highest desire
   And moves but souls that move in Pleasure's rest :
The heavenly charm that lullabies our woes,
   And recollects the mind that cares distract,
The lively death of joyless thoughts o'erthrows,
   And brings rare joys but thought on into act :
Which like the Soul of all the world doth move,
   The universal nature of this All :
The life of life, and soul of joy and love,
   High rapture's heaven : the That I can not call
(Like God) by real name : and what is this
But Music, next the Highest, the highest bliss ?

THE SHOOTING STAR

SO shoots a Star as doth my Mistress glide
   At midnight through my chamber, which she makes
Bright as the sky when moon and stars are spied,
   Wherewith my sleeping eyes amazèd wake :
Which ope no sooner than herself she shuts
Out of my sight, away so fast she flies :

Which me in mind of my slack service puts ;
For which all night I wake, to plague mine eyes.
Shoot, Star ! once more, and if I be thy mark
Thou shalt hit me, for thee I 'll meet withal.
Let mine eyes once more see thee in the dark !
Else they with ceaseless waking out will fall :
And if again such time and place I lose
To close with thee, let mine eyes never close.

LOVE'S BLAZONRY

WHEN I essay to blaze my lovely Love
And to express her all in colours quaint.
I rob earth, sea, air, fire, and all above.
Of their best parts, but her worst parts to paint :
Staidness from earth, from sea the clearest part,
From air her subtlety, from fire her light ;
From sun, moon, stars, the glory they impart :.
So rob and wrong I all, to do her right.
But if the beauty of her mind I touch,
Since that before touch'd touch but parts externe,
I ransack heaven a thousand times as much :
Since in that mind we may that Mind discern,
That all in All that are or fair or good.
And so She 's most divine, in flesh and blood.

AN HELLESPONT OF CREAM

IF there were, O ! an Hellespont of cream
Between us, milk-white Mistress ! I would swim
To you, to show to both my love's extreme,

Leander-like,— yea ! dive from brim to brim.
But met I with a butter'd pippin-pie
Floating upon 't, that would I make my boat
To waft me to you without jeopardy :
Though sea-sick I might be while it did float.
Yet if a storm should rise, by night or day,
Of sugar-snows or hail of care-aways,
Then, if I found a pancake in my way,
It like a plank should bear me to your quays.
Which having found, if they tobacco kept,
The smoke should dry me well before I slept.

THOMAS NASH

FAIR SUMMER

FAIR Summer droops, droop men and beasts therefore !
So fair a Summer never look for more !
All good things vanish less than in a day :
Peace, plenty, pleasure, suddenly decay.
Go not yet hence, bright soul of the sad year !
The earth is hell when thou leavest to appear.

What ! shall those flowers that deck'd thy garland erst
Upon thy grave be wastefully dispersed ?
O trees ! consume your sap in sorrow's source ;
Streams ! turn to tears your tributary course.
Go not yet hence, bright soul of the sad year !
The earth is hell when thou leavest to appear.

GERVASE MARKHAM

SIMPLES

COME BUY, you lusty gallants !
    These simples which I sell !
In all your days were never seen like these,
    For beauty, strength, and smell.
Here 's the king-cup, the pansy with the violet,
    The rose that loves the shower,
    The wholesome gilliflower,
    Both the cowslip, lily,
    And the daffodilly,
    With a thousand in my power.

    Here 's golden amaranthus
      That true love can provoke,
Of horehound store, and poisoning hellebore,
    With the polipode of the oak ;
Here 's chaste vervain, and lustful eringo,
    Health-preserving sage,
    And rue which cures old age ;
    With a world of others,
    Making fruitful mothers :
    All these attend me as my page.

JOHN DONNE

THE FUNERAL

WHOEVER comes to shroud me, do not harm
      Nor question much
That subtle wreath of hair about mine arm !
The mystery, the sign you must not touch :
      For 'tis my outward soul,
Viceroy to that which, then to heaven being gone,
      Will leave this to controul
And keep these limbs, her provinces, from dissolution.

For if the sinewy thread my brain lets fall
      Through every part
Can tie those parts and make me one of all,
Those hairs, which upward grew and strength and art
      Have from a better brain,
Can better do 't : except she mean'd that I
      By this should know my pain,
As prisoners then are manacled, when they 're
               condemn'd to die.

Whate'er she mean'd by 't, bury it with me !
      For since I am
Love's Martyr, it might breed idolatry
If into other hands these relics came.
      As 'twas humility
T" afford to it all that a soul can do,
      So 'tis some bravery
That, since you would have none of me, I bury
               some of you.

THE UNDERTAKING

I HAVE DONE one braver thing
  Than all the Worthies did ;
And yet a braver thence doth spring,
  Which is, to keep that hid.

It were but madness now to impart
  The skill of specular stone,
When he, which can have learn'd the art
  To cut it, can find none.

So, if I now should utter this,
  Others, because no more
Such stuff to work upon there is,
  Would love but as before.

But he, who loveliness within
  Hath found, all outward loathes :
For he, who colour loves and skin,
  Loves but their oldest clothes.

If, as I have, you also do
  Virtue in woman see,
And dare love that, and say so too,
  And forget the HE and SHE,—

And if this love, though placèd so,
  From profane men you hide,
Which will no faith on this bestow
  Or, if they do, deride,—

Then you have done a braver thing
Than all the Worthies did ;
And a braver thence will spring,
Which is, to keep that hid.

BREAK OF DAY

STAY, O SWEET ! and do not rise !
The light that shines comes from thine eyes :
The day breaks not ; it is my heart,
Because that you and I must part.
Stay ! or else my joys will die,
And perish in their infancy.

'Tis true, 'tis day : what though it be ?
O wilt thou therefore rise from me ?
Why should we rise because 'tis light ?
Did we lie down because 'twas night ?
Love, which in spite of darkness brought us hither,
Should in despite of light keep us together.

Light hath no tongue, but is all eye :
If it could speak as well as spy,
This were the worst that it could say,
That being well I fain would stay,
And that I loved my heart and honour so
That I would not from him that had them go.

Must business thee from hence remove ?
Oh, that 's the worst disease of love.
The poor, the false, the foul, love can
Admit, but not the busied man.
He which hath business, and makes love, doth do
Such wrong as when a married man should woo.

EPITHALAMION

UP! youths and virgins! up, and praise
The God whose nights outshine his days!
    Hymen, whose hallow'd rites
    Could never boast of brighter lights,
        Whose bonds pass liberty.
Two of your troop, that with the morn were free,
        Are now waged to his war;
          And what they are,
        If you 'll perfection see,
          Yourselves must be.
Shine, Hesperus! shine forth, thou wished star!

    What joy or honours can compare
    With holy nuptials, when they are
        Made out of equal parts
    Of years, of states, of hands, of hearts;
        When in the happy choice
The spouse and spousèd have the foremost voice?
        Such, glad of Hymen's war,
          Live what they are
        And long perfection see:
          And such ours be.
Shine, Hesperus! shine forth, thou wished star!

The solemn state of this one night
Were fit to last an age's light ;
  But there are rites behind
  Have less of state and more of kind :
   Love's wealthy crop of kisses,
And fruitful harvest of his mother's blisses.
    Sound then to Hymen's war !
    That what these are,
    Who will perfection see
    May haste to be.
Shine, Hesperus ! shine forth, thou wished star !

Love's Commonwealth consists of toys ;
His Council are those antic boys,
   Games, Laughter, Sports, Delights,
That triumph with him on these nights :
   To whom we must give way,
For now their reign begins, and lasts till day.
    They sweeten Hymen's war,
    And in that jar
    Make all, that married be,
    Perfection see.
Shine, Hesperus ! shine forth, thou wished star !

Why stays the bridegroom to invade
Her that would be a matron made ?
   Good-night ! whilst yet we may
  Good-night to you a virgin say.
   To-morrow rise the same
Your mother is, and use a nobler name !
    Speed well in Hymen's war,
    That what you are,

By your perfection, we
And all may see !
Shine, Hesperus ! shine forth, thou wished star !

To-night is Venus' vigil kept,
This night no bridegroom ever slept ;
And if the fair bride do,
The married say 'tis his fault too.
Wake then, and let your lights
Wake too, for they 'll tell nothing of your nights,
But that in Hymen's war
You perfect are ;
And such perfection we
Do pray should be.
Shine, Hesperus ! shine forth, thou wished star !

That, ere the rosy-finger'd Morn
Behold nine moons, there may be born
A babe to uphold the fame
Of Ratcliffe's blood and Ramsay's name ;
That may, in his great seed,
Wear the long honours of his father's deed.
Such fruits of Hymen's war
Most perfect are :
And all perfection we
Wish you should see.
Shine, Hesperus ! shine forth, thou wished star !

IF I FREELY MAY DISCOVER
 What would please me in my lover:
I would have her fair and witty,
Savouring more of Court than City;
A little proud, but full of pity;
Light and humorous in her toying,
Oft building hopes, and soon destroying,
Long but sweet in the enjoying:
Neither too easy nor too hard,
All extremes I would have barr'd.

She should be allow'd her passions,
So they were but used as fashions:
Sometimes froward, and then frowning;
Sometimes sickish, and then swouning;
Every fit with change still crowning:
Purely jealous I would have her,
Then only constant when I crave her:
'Tis a virtue should not save her.
Thus, nor her delicates would cloy me,
Nor her peevishness annoy me.

HER MAN

OF your trouble, BEN! to ease me,
 I will tell what man would please me.

I would have him, if I could,
Noble, or of greater blood,—
Titles, I confess, do take me,
And a woman God did make me;
French to boot, at least in fashion,

And his manners of that nation.
Young I 'd have him too, and fair,
Yet a man ; with crisped hair,
Cast in thousand snares and rings
For Love's fingers and his wings,
Chestnut colour,— or, more slack,
Gold upon a ground of black ;
Venus' and Minerva's eyes,
For he must look wanton-wise ;
Eye-brows bent like Cupid's bow ;
Front an ample field of snow ;
Even nose ; and cheeks withal
Smooth as is the billiard-ball ;
Chin as woolly as the peach ;
And his lip should kissing teach,
Till he cherish'd too much beard
And made love, or me, afear'd.
He should have a hand as soft
As the down, and show it oft ;
Skin as smooth as any rush,
And so thin to see a blush
Rising through it, ere it came ;
All his blood should be a flame
Quickly fired, as in beginners
In Love's school, and yet no sinners.
'Twere too long to speak of all :
What we harmony do call
In a body should be there ;
Well he should his clothes too wear,
Yet no tailor help to make him,—
Dress'd, you still for a man should take him.

And not think he had eat a stake
Or were set up in a brake.
Valiant he should be, as fire
Showing danger more than ire ;
Bounteous as the clouds to earth ;
And as honest as his birth ;
All his actions to be such
As to do no thing too much,—
Nor o'erpraise nor yet condemn,
Nor out-value nor contemn,
Nor do wrongs nor wrongs receive,
Nor tie knots nor knots unweave ;
And from baseness to be free,
As he durst love Truth and Me.

Such a man. with every part,
I could give my very heart :
But of one if short he came,
I can rest me where I am.

IN THE PERSON OF WOMANKIND

MEN ! if you love us, play no more
The fools or tyrants with your friends,
To make us still sing o'er and o'er
Our own false praises, for your ends :
We have both wits and fancies too ;
And if we must, let's sing of you !

Nor do we doubt but that we can,
If we would search with care and pain,
Find some one good in some one man ;
So, going thorough all your strain,

We shall at last of parcels make
One good enough — for a song's sake.

And as a cunning painter takes,
    In any curious piece you see,
More pleasure while the thing he makes
    Than when 'tis made, why so will we :
And having pleased our art we 'll try
To make a new, and hang that by.

BEGGING ANOTHER

FOR LOVE'S SAKE kiss me once again !
    I long and should not beg in vain ;
    Here 's none to spy thee :
        Why do you doubt or stay?
    I 'll taste as lightly as the bee,
That doth but touch his flower and flies away.

One more ! and, 'faith, I will be gone :
Can he that loves ask less than one?
    Nay ! you may err in this
        And all your bounty wrong :
    This could be call'd but half a kiss ;
What were but once to do we should do long.

I will but mend the last, and tell
Where, how, it would have relish'd well ;
    Join lip to lip, and try !
        Each suck the other's breath,
    And whilst our tongues perplexed lie
Let who will think us dead, or wish our death.

SONG OF SATYRS

A CATCH

BUZZ! quoth the Blue-Fly,
   Hum! quoth the Bee;
Buzz and hum! they cry,
      And so do we.
In his ear! in his nose!
Thus,—do you see?

They tickle them.

He eat the Dormouse ——
      Else it was he.

HER GLOVE

THOU more than most sweet Glove
   Unto my more sweet Love!
Suffer me to store with kisses
This empty lodging that now misses
The pure rosy hand that wore thee,
Whiter than the kid that bore thee.
Thou art soft, but that was softer.
Cupid's self hath kiss'd it ofter
Than e'er he did his mother's doves,
Supposing her the Queen of Loves
That was thy mistress, Best of Gloves!

ON MARGARET RATCLIFFE

MARBLE ! weep, for thou dost cover
A dead beauty underneath thee,
Rich as Nature could bequeath thee :
Grant then no rude hand remove her !
All the gazers on the skies
Read not in fair heaven's story
Expresser truth or truer glory
Than they might in her bright eyes.

Rare as wonder was her wit,
And like nectar overflowing ;
Till Time, strong by her bestowing,
Conquer'd hath both life and it :
Life whose grief was out of fashion
In these times. Few so have rued
Fate in another. To conclude,—
For wit, feature, and true passion,
Earth ! thou hast not such another.

HIS EXCUSE FOR LOVING

LET IT NOT your wonder move,
Less your laughter, that I love,
Though I now write fifty years :
I have had and have my peers.
Poets, though divine, are men ;
Some have loved as old again.
And it is not always face,
Clothes, or fortune, gives the grace,

Or the feature, or the youth ;
But the language, and the truth
With the ardour and the passion,
Gives the lover weight and fashion.
If you then will read the story,
First prepare you to be sorry
That you never knew till now
Either whom to love or how ;
But be glad as soon, with me,
When you know that this is She
Of whose beauty it was sung,—
She shall make the old man young,
Keep the middle age at stay,
And let nothing high decay,
Till She be the reason why
All the world for love may die.

SONG OF NIGHT

BREAK, Phantasy ! from thy cave of cloud
    And spread thy purple wings,—
Now all thy figures are allow'd,
    And various shapes of things :
Create of airy forms a stream !
    It must have blood, and nought of phlegm ;
And though it be a waking dream,
CHORUS — Yet let it like an odour rise
    To all the senses here,
And fall like sleep upon their eyes
    Or music in their ear.

FRANCIS AND WALTER DAVISON

TO URANIA — FOR PARDON

SWEET! I do not pardon crave,
　　　Till I have
By deserts this fault amended :
This, I only this desire,
　　　That your ire
May with penance be suspended.

Not my will, but Fate, did fetch
　　　Me, poor wretch,
Into this unhappy error :
Which to plague, no tyrant's mind
　　　Pain can find
Like my heart's self-guilty terror.

Then, O then, let that suffice !
　　　Your dear eyes
Need not, need not more afflict me ;
Nor your sweet tongue, dipp'd in gall,
　　　Need at all
From your presence interdict me.

Unto him that Hell sustains
　　　No new pains

Need be sought for his tormenting :
O, my pains Hell's pains surpass ;
  Yet, alas !
You are still new pains inventing.

By my love, long, firm, and true,
  Borne to you,—
By these tears my grief expressing,—
By this pipe, which nights and days
  Sounds your praise,—
Pity me, my fault confessing !

Or, if I may not desire
  That your ire
May with penance be suspended,
Yet let me full pardon crave
  When I have
With soon death my fault amended.

URANIA'S ANSWER

IN INVERTED RHYMES — STAFF FOR STAFF

SINCE true penance hath suspended
  Feigned ire,
More I 'll grant than you desire.
Faults confess'd are half amended ;
  And I have,
In this half, all that I crave.

Therefore banish now the terror
  Which you find
In your guiltless grievèd mind !

For, though you have made an error,
From me, wretch,
First beginning it did fetch.

Ne'er my sight I 'll interdict thee
More at all;
Ne'er speak words more dipp'd in gall;
Ne'er, ne'er will I more afflict thee
With these eyes:
What is past shall now suffice.

Now new joys I 'll be inventing,
Which, alas!
May thy passed woes surpass.
Too long thou hast felt tormenting;
Too great pains
So great love and faith sustains.

Let these eyes, by thy confessing
Worthy praise,
Never see more nights nor days,—
Let my woes be past expressing,—
When to you
I cease to be kind and true!

Thus are both our states amended:
For you have
Fuller pardon than you crave;
And my fear is quite suspended,
Since mine ire
Wrought the effect I most desire.

UPON HER PROTESTING

THAT SHE LOVED HIM

LADY ! you are with beauties so enriched,
        Of body and of mind,
        As I can hardly find
Which of them all hath most my heart bewitched.

Whether your skin so white, so smooth, so tender,
        Or face so lovely fair,
        Or heart-ensnaring hair,
Or dainty hand, or leg and foot so slender.

Or whether your sharp wit and lively spirit,
        Where pride can find no place,
        Or your most pleasing grace,
Or speech, which doth true eloquence inherit.

Most lovely all, and each of them doth move me
        More than words can express ;
        But yet I must confess
I love you most because you please to love me.

ONLY SHE PLEASES HIM

PASSION may my judgment blear,
   Therefore sure I will not swear
     That others are not pleasing :
But (I speak it to my pain
And my life shall it maintain)
     None else yields my heart easing.

Ladies I do think there be,
Other some as fair as she,
     Though none have fairer features ;
But my turtle-like affection,
Since of her I made election,
     Scorns other fairest creatures.

Surely I will not deny
But some others reach as high
     With their sweet warbling voices ;
But, since her notes charm'd mine ear,
Even the sweetest tunes I hear
     To me seem rude harsh noises.

A COMPARISON

SOME THERE ARE as fair to see too,
   But by art and not by nature ;
Some as tall, and goodly be too,
   But want beauty to their stature ;
Some have gracious, kind behaviour,
   But are foul or simple creatures ;

76 DAVISON

Some have wit, but want sweet favour,
  Or are proud of their good features:
Only you — and you want pity —
Are most fair, tall, kind, and witty.

TO CUPID

LOVE! if a God thou art,
    Then evermore thou must
    Be merciful and just:
If thou be just, O wherefore doth thy dart
Wound mine alone, and not my Lady's heart?

If merciful, then way
    Am I to pain reserved
    Who have thee truly served,
While she that by thy power sets not a fly
Laughs thee to scorn and lives at liberty?

Then if a God thou wilt accounted be,
Heal me like her, or else wound her like me!

BEAUMONT AND FLETCHER

TELL ME!

He — TELL me, Dearest ! what is love?
She — 'Tis a lightning from above ;
    'Tis an arrow ; 'tis a fire ;
    'Tis a boy they call Desire.
  Both — 'Tis a grave
      Gapes to have
  Those poor fools that long to prove.

He — Tell me more !   Are women true?
She — Yes ! some are ; and some as you.
    Some are willing, some are strange.
    Since you men first taught to change.
  Both — And till troth
      Be in both
  All shall love to love anew.

He — Tell me more yet !   Can they grieve?
She — Yes ! and sicken sore, but live,
    And be wiser and delay
    When you men are wise as they.
  Both — Then I see
      Faith will be
  Never till they both believe.

WEDDING SONG

HOLD BACK thy hours, dark Night! till we have done:
            The day will come too soon.
Young maids will curse thee if thou stealest away
And leavest their losses open to the day.
                Stay! stay, and hide
                The blushes of the bride!

Stay, gentle Night! and with thy darkness cover
            The kisses of her lover!
Stay, and confound her tears and her shrill cryings,
Her weak denials, vows, and often dyings!
                Stay, and hide all;
                But help not, though she call!

FREEDOM IN LOVE

NEVER MORE will I protest
            To love a woman, but in jest:
For as they can not be true,
So to give each man his due,
When the wooing fit is past
Their affection can not last.

Therefore, if I chance to meet
With a mistress fair and sweet,
She my service shall obtain,
Loving her, for love again:
This much liberty I crave,—
Not to be a constant slave.

But, when we have tried each other,
If she better like another,
Let her quickly change ! for me
Then to change I am as free.
He or She that loves too long
Sell their freedom for a song.

TRUE BEAUTY

MAY I FIND a woman fair,
And her mind as clear as air !
If her beauty go alone,
'Tis to me as if 'twere none.

May I find a woman rich,
And not of too high a pitch !
If that pride should cause disdain,
Tell me, Lover ! where 's thy gain.

May I find a woman wise,
And her falsehood not disguise !
Hath she wit as she hath will,
Double-arm'd she is to kill.

May I find a woman kind,
And not wavering like the wind !
How should I call that love mine
When 'tis his, and his, and thine ?

May I find a woman true !
There is beauty's fairest hue :
There is beauty, love, and wit.
Happy he can compass it !

HYMN TO PAN

SING HIS PRAISES, that doth keep
  Our flocks from harm,
Pan, the father of our sheep;
  And, arm in arm,
Tread we softly in a round,
While the hollow neighbouring ground
Fills the music with her sound.

Pan! O great god Pan! to thee
  Thus do we sing:
Thou that keep'st us chaste and free
  As the young Spring.
Ever be thy honour spoke,
From that place where Morning broke
To that place Day doth unyoke!

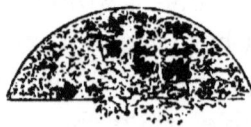

SONG FOR A DANCE

SHAKE OFF your heavy trance!
  And leap into a dance
Such as no mortals use to tread:
  Fit only for Apollo
To play to, for the Moon to lead,
  And all the Stars to follow.

THE ABSTRACT OF MELANCHOLY

WHEN I go musing all alone,
    Thinking of divers things foreknown,
When I build castles in the air,
Void of sorrow and void of fear,
Pleasing myself with phantasms sweet,
Methinks the time runs very fleet.
All my joys to this are folly :
Nought so sweet as melancholy !

When I lie waking, all alone,
Recounting what I have ill done,
My thoughts on me then tyrannize,
Fear and sorrow me surprize :
Whether I tarry still or go,
Methinks the time moves very slow.
All my griefs to this are jolly :
Nought so sad as melancholy !

When to myself I act, and smile,
With pleasing thoughts the time beguile.
By a brook-side or wood so green,
Unheard, unsought for, or unseen,

A thousand pleasures do me bless
And crown my soul with happiness.
All my joys besides are folly :
Nought so sweet as melancholy !

When I lie, sit, or walk alone,
I sigh, I grieve, making great moan,
In a dark grove, or irksome den,
With discontents and furies,— then
A thousand miseries at once
Mine heavy heart and soul ensconce.
All my griefs to this are jolly :
None so sour as melancholy !

Methinks I hear, methinks I see,
Sweet music, wondrous melody,
Towns, palaces, and cities fine,—
Here now, then there, the world is mine ;
Rare beauties, gallant ladies shine,
Whate'er is lovely or divine.
All other joys to this are folly :
None so sweet as melancholy !

Methinks I hear, methinks I see,
Ghosts, goblins, fiends,— my phantasy
Presents a thousand ugly shapes,
Headless bears, black men, and apes ;
Doleful outcries, fearful sights,
My sad and dismal soul affrights.
All my griefs to this are jolly :
None so damn'd as melancholy !

Methinks I court, methinks I kiss,
Methinks I now embrace my Miss:
O blessed days! O sweet content!
In Paradise my time is spent.
Such thoughts may still my fancy move:
So may I ever be in love!
All my joys to this are folly:
Nought so sweet as melancholy!

When I recount love's many frights,
My sighs and tears, my waking nights,
My jealous fits,— O mine hard fate!
I now repent, but 'tis too late.
No torment is so bad as love,
So bitter to my soul can prove.
All my griefs to this are jolly:
Nought so harsh as melancholy!

Friends and companions! get you gone!
'Tis my desire to be alone:
Ne'er well but when my thoughts and I
Do domineer in privacy.
No gem, no treasure like to this,
'Tis my delight, my crown, my bliss.
All my joys to this are folly:
Nought so sweet as melancholy!

'Tis my sole plague to be alone:
I am a beast, a monster grown;
I will no light nor company,
I find it now my misery:

The scene is turn'd, my joys are gone,
Fear, discontent, and sorrows come.
All my griefs to this are jolly :
Nought so fierce as melancholy !

I 'll not change life with any king,
I ravish'd am : can the world bring
More joy than still to laugh and smile,
In pleasant toys time to beguile?
Do not, O do not trouble me !
So sweet content I feel and see.
All my joys to this are folly :
None so divine as melancholy !

I 'll change my state with any wretch
Thou canst from jail or dunghill fetch ;
My pain past cure, another hell,
I may not in this torment dwell.
Now, desperate, I hate my life ;
Lend me a halter or a knife !
All my griefs to this are jolly :
Nought so damn'd as melancholy !

WILLIAM DRUMMOND

SEXTAIN

SITH gone is my delight and only pleasure,
  The last of all my hopes, the cheerful sun
That clear'd my life's dark day, Nature's sweet treasure,
More dear to me than all beneath the moon,
What resteth now but that upon this mountain
I weep till heaven transform me to a fountain?

Fresh, fair, delicious, crystal, pearly fountain,
On whose smooth face to look She oft took pleasure!
Tell me (so may thy streams long cheer this mountain,
So serpent ne'er thee stain, nor scorch thee sun,
So may with gentle beams thee kiss the moon!)
Dost thou not mourn to want so fair a treasure?

While She her glass'd in thee rich Tagus' treasure
Thou envy needed not, nor yet the fountain
In which the hunter saw the naked Moon;
Absence hath robb'd thee of thy wealth and pleasure.
And I remain like marigold, of sun
Deprived, that dies, by shadow of some mountain.

Nymphs of the forests, nymphs who on this mountain
Are wont to dance, showing your beauty's treasure
To goat-feet Sylvans and the wondering Sun!
Whenas you gather flowers about this fountain,

Bid Her farewell who placèd here her pleasure ;
And sing her praises to the stars and moon !

Among the lesser lights as is the Moon,
Blushing through scarf of clouds on Latmos mountain
Or when her silver locks she looks for pleasure
In Thetis' stream proud of so gay a treasure,
Such was my Fair when she sat by this fountain,
With other nymphs, to shun the amorous Sun.

As is our earth in absence of the sun,
Or when of sun deprivèd is the moon,
As is without a verdant shade a fountain,
Or wanting grass a mead, a vale, a mountain,—
Such is my state, bereft of my dear treasure,
To know whose only worth was all my pleasure.

Ne'er think of pleasure, heart !— eyes ! shun the sun ;
Tears be your treasure, which the wandering moon
Shall see you shed, by mountain, vale, and fountain.

DEATH NOT FEARED

I FEAR NOT henceforth death,
Sith after this departure yet I breathe.
Let rocks and seas and wind
Their highest treasons show ;
Let sky and earth combined
Strive if they can to end my life and woe !
Sith grief can not, me nothing can o'erthrow.
Or if that aught can cause my fatal lot,
It will be when I hear I am forgot.

MADRIGAL

SWEET ROSE ! whence is this hue
Which doth all hues excel?
Whence this most fragrant smell?
And whence this form and gracing grace in you?
In flowery Pœstum's field perhaps ye grew,
Or Hybla's hills you bred,
Or odoriferous Enna's plains you fed,
.Or Tmolus, or where boar young Adon slew.
Or hath the Queen of Love you dyed of new
In that dear blood, which makes you look so red?
No ! none of these, but cause more high you bliss'd :
My Lady's breast you bare, and lips you kiss'd.

PLEASANT DEATH

DEAR LIFE ! while I do touch
These coral ports of bliss,
Which still themselves do kiss
And sweetly me invite to do as much,
All panting in my lips
My heart my sense doth leave,
No sense my senses have,
And inward powers do find a strange eclipse.
This death so heavenly well
Doth so me please, that I
Would never longer seek in sense to dwell,
If that even thus I only could but die.

MADRIGAL

A DÆDAL of my death —
  I semble now that subtle worm uneath :
Which, prone to its own ill, can take no rest :
For, with strange thoughts possess'd,
    I feed on fading leaves
    Of hope, which me deceives
And thousand webs doth warp within my breast.
And thus in end unto myself I weave
A fast-shut prison —— No ! but even a grave.

NATHANIEL FIELD

MATIN SONG

R ISE, Lady Mistress ! rise !
  The night hath tedious been ;
No sleep hath fallen into mine eyes,
    Nor slumbers made me sin.
Is not She a saint then, say !
Thought of whom keeps sin away?

Rise Madam ! rise, and give me light,
    Whom darkness still will cover
And ignorance, more dark than night,
    Till thou smile on thy lover.
All want day till thy beauty rise :
For the grey morn breaks from thine eyes.

JOHN WEBSTER

DIRGE

HARK! now every thing is still,
The screech-owl and the whistler shrill
Call upon our Dame aloud,
And bid her quickly don her shroud.
Much you had of land and rent,—
Your length in clay's now competent;
A long war disturb'd your mind,—
Here your perfect peace is sign'd.
Of what is 't fools make such vain keeping?
Sin their conception, their birth weeping,
Their life a general mist of error,
Their death a hideous storm of terror.
Strew your hair with powders sweet ;
Don clean linen ; bathe your feet ;
And (the foul fiend more to check)
A crucifix let bless your neck !
'Tis now full tide 'tween night and day :
End your groan and come away !

WILLIAM BROWNE

VENUS AND ADONIS

VENUS by Adonis' side
  Crying kiss'd and kissing cried ;
Wrung her hands and tore her hair
For Adonis dying there.

Stay ! quoth she : O stay and live !
Nature surely doth not give
To the earth her sweetest flowers
To be seen but some few hours.

On his face, still as he bled,
For each drop a tear she shed,
Which she kiss'd or wiped away,—
Else had drown'd him where he lay.

Fair Proserpina, quoth she,
Shall not have thee yet from me ;
Nor thy soul to fly begin
While my lips can keep it in.

Here she closed again.   And some
Say — Apollo would have come
To have cured his wounded limb,—
But that she had smother'd him.

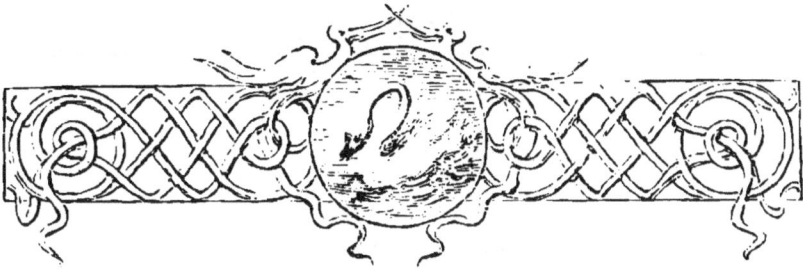

ROBERT HERRICK

THE TEAR

GLIDE, gentle Stream ! and bear
   Along with you my tear
    To that coy Girl
Who smiles, yet slays
Me with delays,
   And strings my tears as pearl.

See ! see ! She 's yonder set,
Making a carcanet
   Of maiden flowers :
There, there present
This orient
   And pendant pearl of ours !

Then say I 've sent one more
Gem to enrich her store ;
   And that is all
Which I can send
Or vainly spend,
   For tears no more will fall.

Nor will I seek supply
Of them, the springs once dry ;
   But I 'll devise

(Among the rest)
A way that 's best
   How I may save mine eyes.

Yet say, should She condemn
Me to surrender them,—
   Then say, my part
Must be to weep
Out them, to keep
   A poor yet loving heart.

Say too, She would have this :
She shall.   Then my hope is
   That, when I 'm poor,
And nothing have
To send or save,
   I 'm sure She 'll ask no more.

SWEET AMARYLLIS

SWEET AMARYLLIS, by a spring's
  Soft and soul-melting murmurings
Slept ; and, thus sleeping, thither flew
A Robin Red-breast, who at view,
Not seeing her at all to stir,
Brought leaves and moss to cover her.
But while he, perking, there did pry,
About the arch of either eye
The lid began to let out day :
At which poor Robin flew away ;
And seeing her not dead, but all disleaved,
He chirp'd for joy to see himself deceived.

PANSIES

FROLIC VIRGINS once these were,
    Over-loving, living here,—
Being here their ends denied,
Ran for Sweethearts mad, and died.
Love, in pity of their tears,
And their loss in blooming years,
For their restless here-spent hours
Gave them hearts' ease, turn'd to Flowers.

TO DAISIES

SHUT NOT so soon! the dull-eyed Night
    Has not as yet begun
To make a seizure on the light
    Or to seal up the sun.

No marigolds yet closèd are,
    No shadows great appear,
Nor doth the early shepherd's star
    Shine like a spangle here.

Stay but until my Julia close
    Her life-begetting eye :
And let the whole world then dispose
    Itself to live or die.

LOVE MAKES ALL LOVELY

WHAT I FANCY I approve :
   No dislike there is in love.
Be my Mistress short or tall,
And distorted therewithal,
Be She likewise one of those
That an acre hath of nose,
Be her forehead and her eyes
Full of incongruities,
Be her cheeks so shallow too
As to show her tongue wag through,
Be her lips ill hung or set,
And her grinders black as jet,
Hath She thin hair, hath She none,
She 's to me a paragon.

A VALENTINE

CHOOSE ME your Valentine !
   Next, let us marry !
Love to the death will pine
   If we long tarry.

Promise and keep your vows,
   Or vow you never !
Love's doctrine disallows
   Troth-breakers ever.

You have broke promise twice,
   Dear ! to undo me ;
If you prove faithless thrice,
   None then will woo ye.

TO WATER-NYMPHS ▲

DRINKING AT A FOUNTAIN

REACH with your whiter hands to me
   Some crystal of the spring !
And I about the cup shall see
   Fresh lilies flourishing.

Or else, sweet Nymphs ! do you but this :
   To the glass your lips incline,
And I shall see by that one kiss
   The water turn'd to wine.

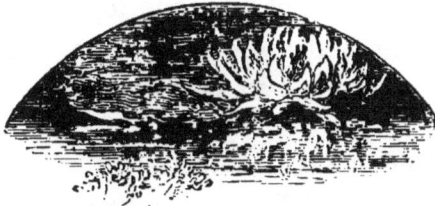

TO ELECTRA

I DARE NOT ask a kiss,
   I dare not beg a smile,
Lest having that or this
   I might grow proud the while.

No ! no ! the utmost share
   Of my desire shall be
Only to kiss that air
   That lately kissed thee.

RICHARD BRATHWAITE

A FIG FOR CARE

HAPPY is that state of his
   Who the world takes as it is !
Lose he honour, friendship, wealth,
Lose he liberty or health,
Lose he all that earth can give,
Having nought whereon to live,
So prepared a mind 's in him,
He 's resolved to sink or swim.

Should I aught dejected be
'Cause blind Fortune frowns on me?
Or put finger in the eye
When I see my Damon die?
Or repine such should inherit
More of honours than of merit?
Or put on a sourer face
To see Virtue in disgrace?

Should I weep when I do try
Fickle friends' inconstancy,
Quite discarding mine and me
When they should the firmest be?

Or think much when barren brains
Are possess'd of rich domains,
When in reason it were fit
They had wealth unto their wit?

Should I spend the morn in tears
'Cause I see my neighbour's ears
Stand so slopewise from his head,
As if they were horns instead?
Or to see his wife at once
Branch his brow and break his sconce;
Or to hear her in her spleen
Callet like a butter-quean?

Should I sigh because I see
Laws like spider-webs to be,
Lesser flies there quickly ta'en,
While the great break out again?
Or so many schisms and sects,
Which foul heresy detects,
To suppress the fire of zeal
Both in church and commonweal?

No! there's nought on earth I fear
That may force from me one tear.
Loss of honours, freedom, health;
Or that mortal idol, wealth:
With these babes may grievèd be,
But they have no power o'er me.
Less my substance, less my share
In my fear and in my care.

Thus to love, and thus to live,
Thus to take, and thus to give,
Thus to laugh, and thus to sing,
Thus to mount on pleasure's wing,
Thus to sport, and thus to speed,
Thus to flourish, nourish, feed,
Thus to spend, and thus to spare,
Is to bid a fig for care.

THOMAS GOFFE

TO SLEEP

DROP golden showers, gentle Sleep !
    And all ye Angels of the Night
Which do us in protection keep,
Make this Queen dream of delight !
Morpheus ! kind a little, be
Death's now true image, for 'twill prove
To this poor Queen that thou art he :
Her grave is made i' the bed of Love.
Thus with sweet sweets can Heaven mix gall,
    And marriage turn to funeral.

JAMES SHIRLEY

TO ODELIA

HEALTH to my fair Odelia !   Some that know
　　How many months are past
　Since I beheld thy lovely brow,
　　Would count an age at least ;
　　　But unto me,
　　Whose thoughts are still on thee,
　　　　I vow
By thy black eyes, 'tis but an hour ago.

That Mistress I pronounce but poor in bliss
　　That, when her servant parts,
　Gives not as much with her last kiss
　　As will maintain two hearts
　　　Till both do meet
　　To taste what else is sweet.
　　　　Is 't fit
Time measure love, or our affection it ?

Cherish that heart, Odelia ! that is mine :
　　And if the North thou fear,
　Dispatch but from thy southern clime
　　A sigh, to warm thine here !
　　　But be so kind

To send by the next wind :
'Tis far,
And many accidents do wait on war.

HUE AND CRY

IN LOVE'S NAME you are charged.   O fly,
And make a speedy hue and cry
After a face, which t' other day
Stole my wandering heart away !
To direct you take, in brief,
These few marks to know the thief.
Her hair, a net of beams, would prove
Strong enough to imprison Jove
Dress'd in his eagle's shape ; her brow
Is a spacious field of snow ;
Her eyes so rich, so pure a grey,
Every look creates a day,
And if they close themselves (not when
The sun doth set) 'tis night again ;
In her cheeks are to be seen
Of flowers both the king and queen,
Thither by all the Graces led
And smiling in their nuptial bed ;
On whom, like pretty nymphs, do wait
Her twin-born lips, whose virgin state
They do deplore themselves, nor miss
To blush so often as they kiss
Without a man.   Beside the rest,
You shall know this felon best
By her tongue : for when your ear

Once a harmony shall hear
So ravishing you do not know
Whether you be in heaven or no,
That, that is She. O straight surprize
And bring her unto Love's assize !
But lose no time, for fear that she
Ruin all mankind like me,
Fate and philosophy controul,
And leave the world without a soul.

TO HIS MISTRESS

I WOULD the God of Love would die,
And give his bow and shafts to me :
 I ask no other legacy :
This happy fate I then would prove,
That, since thy heart I can not move
I 'd cure and kill my own with love.

Yet why should I so cruel be,
To kill myself with loving thee,
 And thou a tyrant still to me ?
Perhaps, could'st thou affection show
To me, I should not love thee so,
And that would be my medicine too.

Then choose to love me or deny,
I will not be so fond to die,
 A martyr to thy cruelty :
If thou be'st weary of me, when
Thou art so wise to love again,
Command, and I 'll forsake thee then.

SONG TO HYMEN

WHAT HELP of tongue do they require
    Or use of other art,
Whose hands thus speak their chaste desire
    And grasp each other's heart?

Weak is that chain that 's made of air,
    Our tongues but chase our breath :
When palms thus meet there 's no despair
    To make a double wreath.

Give but a sigh, a speaking look,
    I care not for more noise ;
Or let me kiss your hand — the book,
    And I have made my choice.

TO ONE SAYING SHE WAS OLD

TELL ME NOT Time hath play'd the thief
Upon her beauty ! My belief
Might have been mock'd, and I had been
An heretic, if I had not seen
My Mistress is still fair to me,
And now I all those graces see
That did adorn her virgin brow.
Her eye hath the same flame in 't now,
To kill or save, the chemist's fire
Equally burns,— so my desire ;
Not any rose-bud less within
Her cheek ; the same snow on her chin ;
Her voice that heavenly music bears

First charm'd my soul, and in my ears
Did leave it trembling ; her lips are
The self-same lovely twins they were ;—
After so many years I miss
No flower in all my paradise.
Time ! I despise thy rage and thee :
Thieves do not always thrive, I see.

THE LOOKING-GLASS

WHEN this crystal shall present
    Your beauty to your eye,
Think ! that lovely face was meant
    To dress another by.
For not to make them proud
These glasses are allow'd
    To those are fair,
    But to compare
The inward beauty with the outward grace,
And make them fair in soul as well as face.

ON HER DANCING

I STOOD and saw my Mistress dance,
    Silent, and with so fix'd an eye,
Some might suppose me in a trance :
    But being asked why,
By One that knew I was in love,
    I could not but impart
My wonder, to behold her move
So nimbly with a marble heart.

WILLIAM HABINGTON

QUI QUASI FLOS EGREDITUR

FAIR MADAM! you
May see what 's man in yon bright rose :
Though it the wealth of Nature owes,
    It is oppress'd and bends with dew.

Which shows, though Fate
May promise still to warm our lips,
And keep our eyes from an eclipse,
    It will our pride with tears abate.

Poor silly flower !
Though on thy beauty thou presume,
And breath which doth the Spring perfume,
    Thou mayst be cropp'd this very hour.

And though it may
Then thy good fortune be to rest
On the pillow of some Lady's breast,
    Thou 'lt wither and be thrown away.

For 'tis thy doom,
However, that there shall appear
No memory that thou grew'st here,
    Ere the tempestuous winter come.

But flesh is loath
By meditation to foresee
How loathed a nothing it must be,—
   Proud in the triumphs of its growth ;

And tamely can
Behold this mighty world decay
And wear by the age of Time away,
   Yet not discourse the fall of man.

But, Madam ! these
Are thoughts to cure sick human pride ;
And medicines are in vain applied
   To bodies far 'bove all disease.

For you so live
As the Angels, in one perfect state :
Safe from the ruins of our fate
   By virtue's great preservative.

And though we see
Beauty enough to warm each heart,
Yet you, by a chaste chemic art,
   Calcine frail love to piety.

FINE YOUNG FOLLY

FINE young Folly ! though you were
   That fair beauty I did swear,
     Yet you ne'er could reach my heart :
For we courtiers learn at school
Only with your sex to fool ;
     You 're not worth the serious part.

When I sigh and kiss your hand,
Cross my arms and wondering stand,
   Holding parley with your eye ;
Then dilate on my desires,
Swear the sun ne'er shot such fires :
   All is but a handsome lie.

When I eye your curl or lace,
Gentle Soul ! you think your face
   Straight some murder doth commit ;
And your virtue doth begin
To grow scrupulous of my sin,
   When I talk to show my wit.

Therefore, Madam ! wear no cloud,
Nor to check my love grow proud :
   For in sooth I much do doubt
'Tis the powder in your hair,
Not your breath, perfumes the air ;
   And your clothes that set you out.

Yet, though truth has this confess'd,
And I vow I love in jest,
   When I next begin to court
And protest an amorous flame
You will swear I earnest am :—
   Bedlam ! this is pretty sport.

THE PERFECTION OF LOVE

YOU who are earth and can not rise
          Above your sense,
Boasting the envied wealth which lies
Bright in your Mistress' lips or eyes,
          Betray a pitied eloquence.

That which doth join *our* souls so light
          And quick doth move
That, like the eagle in his flight,
It doth transcend all human sight,
          Lost in the element of love.

You poets reach not this who sing
          The praise of dust,
But kneaded, when by theft you bring
The rose and lily from the Spring
          To adorn the wrinkled face of Lust.

When *we* speak love, nor art nor wit
          We gloss upon :
Our souls engender, and beget
Ideas,— which you counterfeit
          In your dull propagation.

While Time seven ages shall disperse
          We 'll talk of love ;
And when our tongues hold no commerce
Our thoughts shall mutually converse,
          And yet the blood no rebel prove.

And though we be of several kind,
     Fit for offence,
Yet are we so by love refined
From impure dross, we are all mind :
Death could not more have conquer'd sense.

How suddenly those flames expire
     Which scorch our clay !
Prometheus-like when we steal fire
From heaven, 'tis endless and entire ;
     It may know age, but not decay.

SIR RICHARD FANSHAWE

OF BEAUTY

LET us use it while we may
   Snatch those joys that haste away !
Earth her winter coat may cast,
And renew her beauty past :
But, our winter come, in vain
We solicit Spring again ;
And when our furrows snow shall cover
Love may return, but never lover.

EDMUND WALLER

TO A FAIR LADY

PLAYING WITH A SNAKE

STRANGE, that such horror and such grace
Should dwell together in one place :
A Fury's arm, an Angel's face !

'Tis innocence, and youth, which makes
In Chloris' fancy such mistakes :
To start at love and play with snakes.

By this and by her coldness barr'd,
Her servants have a task too hard :
The Tyrant has a double guard.

Thrice happy Snake, that in her sleeve
May boldly creep ! we dare not give
Our thoughts so unconfined a leave.

Contented in that nest of snow
He lies, as he his bliss did know ;
And to the wood no more will go.

Take heed, fair Eve ! you do not make
Another tempter of this Snake :
A marble one so warm'd would speak.

TO MY YOUNG LADY LUCY SIDNEY

WHY came I so untimely forth
Into a world which, wanting thee,
Could entertain us with no worth
Or shadow of felicity,
That time should me so far remove
From that which I was born to love?

Yet, Fairest Blossom ! do not slight
That age which you may know so soon :
The rosy morn resigns her light
And milder glory to the noon ;
And then what wonders shall you do
Whose dawning beauty warms us so?

Hope waits upon the flowery prime ;
And Summer, though it be less gay,
Yet is not look'd on as a time
Of declination or decay :
For with a full hand that does bring
All that was promised by the Spring.

AN APOLOGY

FOR HAVING LOVED BEFORE

THEY that never had the use
Of the grape's surprizing juice
To the first delicious cup
All their reason render up :
Neither do nor care to know
Whether it be best or no.

So they that are to love inclined,
　　Sway'd by chance, not choice or art.
To the first that 's fair or kind
　　Make a present of their heart.
'Tis not She that first we love,
But whom dying we approve.

To man, that was in the evening made,
　　Stars gave the first delight,
Admiring in the gloomy shade
　　Those little drops of light ;
Then at Aurora, whose fair hand
　　Removed them from the skies.
He gazing tow'rd the East did stand,
　　She entertain'd his eyes.

But when the bright Sun did appear
　　All those he 'gan despise ;
His wonder was determined there,
　　And could no longer rise :
He neither might nor wish'd to know
　　A more refulgent light,
For that, as mine your beauties now.
　　Employ'd his utmost sight.

TO A LADY

WHO GAVE HIM A LOST COPY OF A POEM

NOTHING lies hid from radiant eyes ;
　　All they subdue become their spies ;
Secrets, as choicest jewels, are
Presented to oblige the Fair :

No wonder then that a lost thought
Should there be found where souls are caught.
   The picture of fair Venus (that
   For which men say the Goddess sat)
   Was lost, till Lely from your look
   Again that glorious image took.
   If Virtue's self were lost, we might
   From your fair mind new copies write.
   All things but one you can restore :
   The heart you get returns no more.

STAY, PHŒBUS!

STAY, Phœbus ! stay !
  The world to which you fly so fast,
    Conveying day
From us to them, can pay your haste
With no such object nor salute your rise
With no such wonder as De Mornay's eyes.

   Well does this prove
   The error of those antique books
    Which made you move
   About the world : Her charming looks
Would fix your beams, and make it ever day,
Did not the rolling earth snatch her away.

SIR JOHN SUCKLING

A BALLAD OF A WEDDING

I TELL thee, DICK ! where I have been,
Where I the rarest things have seen,
   O, things beyond compare !
Such sights again can not be found
In any place on English ground,
   Be it at wake or fair.

At Charing-Cross, hard by the way
Where we, thou know'st, do sell our hay,
   There is a House with stairs ;
And there did I see coming down
Such volk as are not in our town,
   Vorty at least, in pairs.

Amongst the rest One pest'lent fine,
His beard no bigger though than thine,
   Walk'd on before the best :
Our Landlord looks like nothing to him ;
The King, God bless him ! 'twould undo him
   Should he go still so dress'd.

At course-a-park, without all doubt,
He should have first been taken out
   By all the maids i' the town,
Though lusty Roger there had been,

Or little George upon the Green,
  Or Vincent of the Crown.

But wot you what? the Youth was going
To make an end of all his wooing;
  The parson for him stay'd:
Yet by his leave, for all his haste,
He did not so much wish all past,
  Perchance, as did the Maid.

The Maid,—and thereby hangs a tale,
For such a Maid no Widson ale
  Could ever yet produce:
No grape that's kindly ripe could be
So round, so plump, so soft as she,
  Nor half so full of juice.

Her finger was so small the ring
Would not stay on which he did bring,
  It was too wide a peck;
And to say truth, for out it must,
It look'd like the great collar, just,
  About our young colt's neck.

Her feet beneath her petticoat
Like little mice stole in and out,
  As if they fear'd the light;
But, Dick! she dances such a way,
No sun upon an Easter day
  Is half so fine a sight.

He would have kiss'd her once or twice,
But she would not, she was so nice,

She would not do 't in sight;
And then she look'd as who would say
I will do what I list to-day,
    And you shall do 't at night.

Her cheeks so rare a white was on,
No daisy makes comparison,—
    Who sees them is undone :
For streaks of red were mingled there
Such as are on a Katherine pear,
    The side that 's next the sun.

Her lips were red, and one was thin,
. Compared to that was next her chin,—
    Some bee had stung it newly :
But, Dick ! her eyes so guard her face,
I durst no more upon them gaze
    Than on the sun in July.

Her mouth so small, when she does speak,
Thou 'dst swear her teeth her words did break,
    That they might passage get ;
But she so handled still the matter,
They came as good as ours, or better,
    And are not spent a whit.

If wishing should be any sin
The parson himself had guilty been,
    She look'd that day so purely ;
And did the Youth so oft the feat
At night as some did in conceit,
    It would have spoil'd him surely.

Passion o' me ! how I run on :
There 's that that would be thought upon,
    I trow, besides the Bride :
The business of the kitchen 's great,
For it is fit that men should eat ;
    Nor was it there denied.

Just in the nick the cook knock'd thrice,
And all the waiters in a trice
    His summons did obey ;
Each serving-man with dish in hand
March'd boldly up, like our train'd band,
    Presented, and away.

When all the meat was on the table
What man of knife, or teeth, was able
    To stay to be intreated?
And this the very reason was
Before the parson could say grace
    The company was seated.

Now hats fly off, and youths carouse ;
Healths first go round, and then the house,—
    The Bride's came thick and thick ;
And when 'twas named another's health,
Perhaps he made it her's by stealth :
    And who could help it? Dick !

O' the sudden up they rise and dance ;
Then sit again, and sigh, and glance ;
    Then dance again and kiss :
Thus several ways the time did pass,

Whilst every woman wish'd her place,
  And every man wish'd his.

By this time all were stolen aside
To counsel and undress the Bride,
  But that he must not know :
But it was thought he guess'd her mind,
And did not mean to stay behind
  Above an hour or so.

When in he came, Dick ! there she lay
Like new-fall'n snow melting away,—
  'Twas time, I trow, to part :
Kisses were now the only stay,
Which soon she gave, as who would say
  God b' w' y' ! with all my heart.

But just as heavens would have to cross it
In came the bridemaids with the posset ;
  The Bridegroom eat in spite :
For had he left the women to 't,
It would have cost two hours to do 't,
  Which were too much that night.

At length the candle 's out, and now
All that they had not done they do :
  What that is who can tell?
But I believe it was no more
Than thou and I have done before
  With Bridget and with Nell.

LOVING AMISS

HONEST LOVER whosoever !
   If in all thy love there ever
Was one wavering thought, thy flame
Were not still even, still the same,
         Know this :
         Thou lovest amiss
And, to love true,
Thou must begin again and love anew.

If when She appears i' the room
Thou dost not quake and art struck dumb,
   And in striving this to cover
Dost not speak thy words twice over,
         Know this :
         Thou lovest amiss
And, to love true,
Thou must begin again and love anew.

If fondly thou dost not mistake
And all defects for graces take,
Persuade thyself that jests are broken
When she hath little or nought spoken,
         Know this :
         Thou lovest amiss
And, to love true,
Thou must begin again and love anew.

If when thou appear'st to be within
Thou lett'st not men ask and ask again,

And when thou answerest, if it be
To what was ask'd thee properly.
   Know this :
   Thou lovest amiss
And, to love true,
Thou must begin again and love anew.

If when thy stomach calls to eat
Thou cutt'st not fingers 'stead of meat
And, with much gazing on her face,
Dost not rise hungry from thy place,
   Know this :
   Thou lovest amiss
And, to love true,
Thou must begin again and love anew.

If by this thou dost discover
That thou art no perfect lover
And, desiring to love true,
Thou dost begin to love anew,
   Know this :
   Thou lovest amiss
And, to love true,
Thou must begin again and love anew.

A HEALTH

A HEALTH to the nut-brown Lass
 With the hazel eyes ! Let it pass !
  She that hath good eyes
   —— Is a prize.
 Let it pass ! let it pass !

As much to the lively grey :
As good i' the night as day !
   She that hath good eyes,
     Fair and wise ——
Drink away ! drink away !

I pledge, I pledge : what, ho ! some wine !
Here 's to thine —— and to thine ——
   The colours are divine :
But O, to the black ! the black !
Give me as much again, and let it be sack !
    She that hath black eyes
      —— Hath Love's guise
And, it may be, a better knack.

BARLEY-BREAK

LOVE, Reason, Hate, did once bespeak
  Three mates to play at barley-break.
Love Folly took, and Reason Fancy,
And Hate consorts with Pride : so dance they.
   Love coupled last : and so it fell
   That Love and Folly were in Hell.

   They break, and Love would Reason meet,
   But Hate was nimble on her feet ;
   Fancy looks for Pride and thither
   Hies, and they two hug together :
   Yet this new coupling still doth tell
   That Love and Folly were in Hell.

   The rest do break again, and Pride
   Hath now got Reason on her side ;

Hate and Fancy meet, and stand
Untouch'd by Love in Folly's hand :
Folly was dull, though Love ran well :
So Love and Folly were in Hell.

THOMAS NABBES

HER REAL WORTH

WHAT though with figures I should raise
Above all height my Mistress' praise,
Calling her cheek a blushing rose,
The fairest June did e'er disclose,
Her forehead lilies, and her eyes
The luminaries of the skies ;
That on her lips ambrosia grows,
And from her kisses nectar flows?
Too great hyperbolès ! unless
She loves me she is none of these.
But if her heart and her desires
Do answer mine with equal fires,
These attributes are then too poor :
She is all these, and ten times more.

JOSEPH RUTTER

SONG OF VENUS

COME, Lovely Boy! unto my court,
   And leave these uncouth woods and all
   That feed thy fancy with love's gall
But keep away the honey and the sport!
CHORUS OF GRACES — Come unto me!
           And with variety
Thou shalt be fed: which Nature loves, and I.

There is no music in a voice
   That is but one, and still the same :
   Inconstancy is but a name
To fright poor lovers from a better choice.
CHORUS — Come then to me! ——

Orpheus that on Eurydicè
   Spent all his love, on others scorn,
   Now on the banks of Hebrus torn
Finds the reward of foolish constancy.
CHORUS — Come then to me! ——

And sigh no more for one love lost!
   I have a thousand Cupids here
   Shall recompense with better cheer
Thy misspent labours and thy bitter cost.
CHORUS — Come then to me! ——

MARRIAGE HYMN

HYMEN ! God of marriage bed !
Be thou ever honoured :
Thou whose torch's purer light
Death's sad tapers did affright,
And instead of funeral fires
Kindled lovers' chaste desires :
　　May their love
　　Ever prove
True and constant ; let not age
Know their youthful heat to assuage !

Maids ! prepare the genial bed :
Then come, Night ! and hide that red
Which from her cheeks his heart does burn,
Till the envious Day return
And the lusty bridegroom say
— I have chased her fears away,
　　And instead
　　Of virginhed
Given her a greater good,
Perfection and womanhood.

RICHARD CRASHAW

WISHES

TO HIS SUPPOSED MISTRESS

WHOE'ER she be
That not impossible She
That shall command my heart and me ;

Where'er she lie,
Lock'd up from mortal eye,
In shady leaves of destiny :

Till that ripe Birth
Of studied Fate stand forth
And teach her fair steps tread our earth ;

Till that Divine
Idea take a shrine
Of crystal flesh, through which to shine :

Meet her, my Wishes !
Bespeak her to my blisses,
And be you call'd my absent kisses. —

I wish her beauty
That owes not all its duty
To gaudy tire or glistering shoe-tye,—

Something more than
Taffeta or tissue can,
Or rampant feather or rich fan,—

More than the spoil
Of shop, or silkworm's toil,
Or a bought blush, or a set smile ;

A face that 's best
By its own beauty dress'd,
And can alone commend the rest,—

A face made up
Out of no other shop
Than what Nature's white hand sets ope ;

A cheek where youth
And blood, with pen of truth
Write what their reader sweetly ru'th,—

A cheek where grows
More than a morning rose,
Which to no box its being owes ;

Lips where all day
A lover's kiss may play,
Yet carry nothing thence away ;

Looks that oppress
Their richest tires, but dress
Themselves in simple nakedness ;

Eyes that displace
The neighbour diamond and outface
That sun-shine by their own sweet grace ;

Tresses that wear
Jewels, but to declare
How much themselves more precious are,—

Whose native ray
Can tame the wanton day
Of gems that in their bright shades play,—

Each ruby there
Or pearl that dare appear,
Be its own blush, be its own tear;

A well-tamed heart,
For whose more noble smart
Love may be long choosing a dart;

Eyes that bestow
Full quivers on Love's bow,
Yet pay less arrows than they owe;

Smiles that can warm
The blood, yet teach a charm
That chastity shall take no harm;

Blushes that been
The burnish of no sin,
Nor flames of aught too hot within;

Joys that confess
Virtue for their Mistress,
And have no other head to dress;

Fears fond, and flight,
As the coy bride's when night
First does the longing lover right;

Tears quickly fled
And vain, as those are shed
For dying maidenhed;

Days that need borrow
No part of their good morrow
From a fore-spent night of sorrow,—

Days that, in spite
Of darkness, by the light
Of a clear mind are day all night ;

Nights sweet as they
Made short by lovers' play,
Yet long by the absence of the day ;

Life that dares send
A challenge to his end,
And when it comes say — Welcome, friend ;

Sidneian showers
Of sweet discourse, whose powers
Can crown old Winter's head with flowers ;

Soft silken hours,
Open suns, shady bowers ;
'Bove all, nothing within that lours ;

Whate'er delight
Can make Day's forehead bright
Or give down to the wings of Night.

In her whole frame
Have Nature all the name,
Art and Ornament the shame !

Her flattery
Picture and poesy,
Her counsel her own virtue be !

I wish her store
Of worth may leave her poor
Of wishes ; and I wish —— no more.

Now, if Time knows
That Her whose radiant brows
Weave them a garland of my vows,

Her whose just bays
My future hopes can raise
A trophy to her present praise,

Her that dares be
What these lines wish to see,
I seek no further —— it is She.

'Tis She : and here
Lo I unclothe and clear
My Wishes' cloudy character.

May She enjoy it
Whose merit dares apply it
But modesty dares still deny it !

Such Worth as this is
Shall fix my flying wishes,
And determine them to kisses.

Let her full glory,
My fancies ! fly before ye !
Be you my fictions, but Her Story !

RICHARD LOVELACE

THE GRASSHOPPER

To my noble friend — Mr. Charles Cotton

O THOU that swing'st upon the waving ear
   Of some well-filled oaten beard,
Drunk every night with a delicious tear
   Dropp'd thee from heaven, where thou wast rear'd !

The joys of earth and air are thine entire,
   That with thy feet and wings dost hop and fly ;
And when thy poppy works, thou dost retire
   To thy carved acorn-bed to lie.

Up with the day, the sun thou welcomest then,
   Sport'st in the gilt plaits of his beams ;
And all these merry days makest merry men,
   Thyself, and melancholy streams.

But, ah ! the sickle ! golden ears are cropp'd,
   Ceres and Bacchus bid good-night,
Sharp frosty fingers all your flowers have topp'd,
   And what scythes spared winds shave off quite.

Poor verdant fool, and now green ice ! thy joys
   (Large and as lasting as thy perch of grass)
Bid *us* lay in 'gainst winter rains, and poise
   Their floods with an o'erflowing glass.

Thou best of men and friends ! *we* will create
   A genuine summer in each other's breast
And, spite of this cold time and frozen fate,
   Thaw us a warm seat to our rest.

Our sacred hearths shall burn eternally,
   As Vestal flames ; the North-Wind, he
Shall strike his frost-stretch'd wings, dissolve, and fly
   This Ætna in epitome.

Dropping December shall come weeping in,
   Bewail the usurping of his reign ;
But, when in showers of old Greek we begin,
   Shall cry he hath his crown again.

Night, as clear Hesper, shall our tapers whip
   From the light casements where we play,
And the dark hag from her black mantle strip,
   And stick there everlasting day.

Thus richer than untempted kings are we
   That, asking nothing, nothing need.
Though lord of all that seas embrace, yet he
   That wants himself is poor indeed.

SIR EDWARD SHERBURNE

THE HEART-MAGNET

SHALL I, hopeless, then pursue
   A fair shadow that still flies me?
Shall I still adore and woo
   A proud heart that does despise me?
I a constant love may so,
But, alas! a fruitless show.

Shall I by the erring light
   Of two crossing stars still sail,
That do shine, but shine in spite,
   Not to guide but make me fail?
I a wandering course may steer,
But the harbour ne'er come near.

Whilst these thoughts my soul possess
   Reason passion would o'ersway,
Bidding me my flames suppress
   Or divert some other way:
But what reason would pursue,
That my heart runs counter to.

So a pilot, bent to make
   Search for some unfound-out land,

Does with him the magnet take,
  Sailing to the unknown strand :
But that, steer which way he will,
  To the lovèd North points still.

FALSE LYCORIS

LATELY, by clear Thames, his side,
    Fair Lycoris I espied,
With the pen of her white hand
These words printing on the sand :
    None Lycoris doth approve
    But Mirtillo for her love.
Ah, false Nymph ! those words were fit
  In sand only to be writ :
For the quickly rising streams
Of Oblivion and the Thames
In a little moment's stay
From the shore wash'd clean away
What thy hand had there impress'd,
And Mirtillo from thy breast.

ANDREW MARVELL

THE PICTURE OF LITTLE T. C.

In a prospect of flowers.

SEE ! with what simplicity
　This Nymph begins her golden days.
In the green grass she loves to lie,
And there with her fair aspect tames
The wilder flowers, and gives them names :
　　But only with the roses plays,
　　　　And them does tell
What colour best becomes them, and what smell.

Who can foretell for what high cause　·
　This Darling of the Gods was born ?
Yet this is She whose chaster laws
The wanton Love shall one day fear,
And, under her command severe,
　See his bow broke and ensigns torn.
　　　Happy who can
Appease this virtuous enemy of man !

O then let me in time compound ;
　And parley with those conquering eyes
Ere they have tried their force to wound.
Ere with their glancing wheels they drive

In triumph over hearts that strive,
And them that yield but more despise !
Let me be laid
Where I may see the glories from some shade !

Meantime, whilst every verdant thing
Itself does at thy beauty charm,
Reform the errors of the Spring !
Make that the tulips may have share
Of sweetness, seeing they are fair ;
And roses of their thorns disarm ;
But most procure
That violets may a longer age endure !

But O, Young Beauty of the Woods !
Whom Nature courts with fruits and flowers,
Gather the flowers, but spare the buds !
Lest Flora, angry at thy crime
— To kill her infants in their prime,
Should quickly make the example yours ;
And, ere we see,
Nip in the blossom all our hopes in thee.

A DEFINITION OF LOVE

MY LOVE is of a birth as rare
As 'tis for object strange and high :
It was begotten by Despair
Upon Impossibility.

Magnanimous Despair alone
Could show me so divine a thing,

Where feeble Hope could ne'er have flown
But vainly flapp'd its tinsel wing.

And yet I quickly might arrive
Where my extended soul is fix'd :
But Fate does iron wedges drive,
And always crowds itself betwixt.

For Fate with jealous eye doth see
Two perfect loves, nor lets them close :
Their union would her ruin be
And her tyrannic power depose.

And therefore her decrees of steel
Us as the distant poles have placed —
Though Love's whole world on us doth wheel,
Not by themselves to be embraced :

Unless the giddy heaven fall
And earth some new convulsion tear,
And, us to join, the world should all
Be cramp'd into a planisphere.

As lines, so loves oblique may well
Themselves in every angle greet :
But ours, so truly parallel,
Though infinite can never meet.

Therefore the love which us doth bind,
But Fate so enviously debars,
Is the conjunction of the mind
And opposition of the stars.

CLORINDA AND DAMON

CLORINDA

DAMON ! come drive thy flocks this way !

DAMON

No ! 'Tis too late they went astray.

CLORINDA

I have a grassy 'scutcheon spied,
Where Flora blazons all her pride :
The grass I aim to feast thy sheep,
The flowers I for thy temples keep.

DAMON

Grass withers and the flowers too fade.

CLORINDA

Seize the short joys then ere they vade !
Seest thou that unfrequented cave ?

DAMON

That den ?

CLORINDA

Love's shrine.

DAMON

       But virtue's grave.

CLORINDA

In whose cool bosom we may lie,
Safe from the sun.

DAMON

       Not heaven's eye.

CLORINDA

Near this a fountain's liquid bell
Tinkles within the concave shell.

DAMON

Might a soul bathe there and be clean,
Or slake its drought?

CLORINDA

What is 't you mean?

DAMON

Clorinda! pastures, caves, and springs,—
These once had been enticing things.

CLORINDA

And what late change?

DAMON

The other day
Pan met me.

CLORINDA

What did great Pan say?

DAMON

Words that transcend poor shepherd's skill;
But he e'er since my songs does fill,
And his name swells my slender oat.

CLORINDA

Sweet must Pan sound in Damon's note.

DAMON

Clorinda's voice might make it sweet.

CLORINDA

Who would not in Pan's praises meet?

CHORUS

Of Pan the flowery pastures sing !
Caves echo, and the fountains ring.
Sing then while he doth us inspire !
For all the world is our Pan's quire.

THE FAIR SINGER

TO make a final conquest of all me
   Love did compose so sweet an enemy,
In whom both beauties to my death agree,
   Joining themselves in fatal harmony :
That while she with her eyes my heart doth bind
She with her voice might captivate my mind.

I could have fled from One but singly fair.—
   My disentangled soul itself might save,
Breaking the curled trammels of her hair :
   But how should I avoid to be her slave,
Whose subtle art invisibly can wreathe
My fetters of the very air I breathe?

It had been easy fighting in some plain
   Where victory might hang in equal choice,
But all resistance against her is vain
   Who has the advantage both of eyes and voice :
And all my forces needs must be undone,
She having gained both the wind and sun.

MAKING HAY-ROPES

AMETAS

THINK'ST THOU that this love can stand,
   Whilst thou still dost say me Nay?
Love unpaid does soon disband :
   Love binds love, as hay binds hay.

THESTYLIS

Think'st thou that this rope would twine
   If we both should turn one way?
Where both parties so combine
   Neither love will twist nor hay.

AMETAS

Thus you vain excuses find,
   Which yourself and us delay :
And love ties a woman's mind
   Looser than with ropes of hay.

THESTYLIS

What you can not constant hope
Must be taken as you may.

AMETAS

Then let 's both lay by our rope,
And go kiss within the hay !

ALEXANDER BROME

PALINODE

NO MORE, no more of this, I vow !
'Tis time to leave this fooling now,
  Which few but fools call wit.
There was a time when I begun,
And now 'tis time I should have done
  And meddle no more with it :
He physic's use doth quite mistake,
Who physic takes for physic's sake.

My heat of youth, and love, and pride,
Did swell me with their strong spring-tide,
  Inspired my brain and blood ;
And made me then converse with toys
Which are call'd Muses by the boys,
  And dabble in their flood.
I was persuaded in those days
There was no crown like love and bays.

But now my youth and pride are gone,
And age and cares come creeping on,
  And business checks my love :
What need I take a needless toil
To spend my labour, time, and oil,
  Since no design can move?
For now the cause is ta'en away
What reason is 't the effect should stay?

'Tis but a folly now for me
To spend my time and industry
   About such useless wit :
For when I think I have done well,
I see men laugh, but can not tell
   Where 't be at me or it.
Great madness 'tis to be a drudge,
When those that can not write dare judge.

Besides the danger that ensu'th
To him that speaks or writes the truth,
   The premium is so small :
To be call'd Poet and wear bays,
And factor turn of songs and plays,—
   This is no wit at all.
Wit only good to sport and sing
Is a needless and an endless thing.

Give me the wit that can't speak sense,
Nor read it but in 's own defence,
   Ne'er learn'd but of his Gran'am !
He that can buy and sell and cheat
May quickly make a shift to get
   His thousand pound *per annum ;*
And purchase without more ado
The poems, and the poet too.

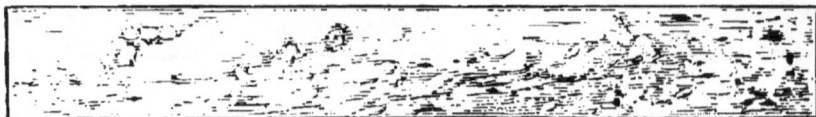

RICHARD BROME

BEGGARS' SONG

COME ! COME AWAY ! the Spring,
By every bird that can but sing
Or chirp a note, doth now invite
Us forth to taste of his delight,
In field, in grove, on hill, in dale ;
But above all the nightingale,
Who in her sweetness strives to outdo
The loudness of the hoarse cuckoo.

Cuckoo ! cries he ; jug, jug, jug ! sings she :
From bush to bush, from tree to tree.
Why in one place then tarry we ?

Come away ! Why do we stay ?
We have no debt or rent to pay ;
No bargains or accompts to make ;
Nor land nor lease, to let or take.
Or if we had, should that remore us
When all the world 's our own before us,
And where we pass and make resort
It is our kingdom and our court.

Cuckoo ! cries he ; jug, jug, jug ! sings she :
From bush to bush, from tree to tree.
Why in one place then tarry we ?

HENRY VAUGHAN

EPITHALAMIUM

TO THE BEST AND MOST ACCOMPLISH'D COUPLE —

BLESSINGS as rich and fragrant crown your heads
　　As the mild heaven on roses sheds
　　When at their cheeks like pearls they wear
　　The clouds that court them in a tear !
　　And may they be fed from above
　　By Him which first ordain'd your love !

　　Fresh as the Hours may all your pleasures be,
　　　　And healthful as Eternity !
　　　　Sweet as the flowers' first breath, and close
　　　　As the unseen spreadings of the Rose
　　　　When she unfolds her curtain'd head
　　　　And makes her bosom the Sun's bed !

　　Soft as yourselves run your whole lives, and clear
　　　　As your own glass, or what shines there !
　　　　Smooth as Heaven's face, and bright as he
　　　　When without mask or tiffany.
　　　　In all your time not one jar meet,—
　　　　But peace as silent as his feet !

　　Like the Day's warmth may all your comforts be,
　　　　Untoil'd for and serene as he,

Yet free and full as is that sheaf
Of sunbeams gilding every leaf
When now the tyrant heat expires
And his cool'd locks breathe milder fires !

And as the parcel'd glories he doth shed
Are the fair issues of his head,
Which, ne'er so distant, are soon known
By the heat and lustre for his own,
So may each branch of yours we see
Your copies and our wonders be !

And when no more on earth you may remain,
Invited hence to heaven again,
Then may your virtuous virgin-flames
Shine in those heirs of your fair names,
And teach the world that mystery —
Yourselves in your posterity !

So you to both worlds shall rich presents bring :
And, gather'd up to heaven, leave here a Spring.

THOMAS STANLEY

SONG

I PRITHEE let my heart alone !
   Since now 'tis raised above thee,
Not all the beauty thou dost own
   Again can make me love thee.

He that was shipwreck'd once before
   By such a Syren's call,
And yet neglects to shun that shore,
   Deserves his second fall.

Each flattering kiss, each tempting smile,
   Thou dost in vain bestow,
Some other lovers might beguile
   Who not thy falsehood know.

But I am proof against all art :
   No vows shall e'er persuade me
Twice to present a wounded heart
   To her that hath betray'd me.

Could I again be brought to love
   Thy form, though more divine,
I might thy scorn as justly move
   As now thou sufferest mine.

NIGHT

CHARISSA — What if Night
    Should betray us, and reveal
      To the light
    All the pleasures that we steal?

PHILOCHARIS — Fairest! we
    Safely may this fear despise :
      How can She
    See our actions, who wants eyes?

CHARISSA — Each dim star,
    And the clearer lights, we know,
      Night's eyes are :
    They were blind that thought her so.

PHILOCHARIS — Those pale fires
    Only burn to yield a light
      To our desires ;
    And, though blind, to give us sight.

CHARISSA — By this shade,
    That surrounds us, might our flame
      Be betray'd,
    And the day disclose its name.

PHILOCHARIS — Dearest Fair !
    These dark witnesses we find
      Silent are :
    Night is dumb as well as blind.

A KISS I BEGG'D, and thou didst join
      Thy lips to mine ;
Then, as afraid, snatch back their treasure
    And mock my pleasure.
Again ! my Dearest ! — for in this
Thou only gavest desire, and not a kiss.

JOHN HALL

EPITAPH

*On a Gentleman and his Wife who died both within
a very few days.*

THRICE happy pair ! who had and have
  Living one bed, now dead one grave :
Whose love being equal, neither could
A life unequal wish to hold ;
But left a question, whether one
Did follow 'cause her mate was gone,
Or the other went before to stay
Till that his fellow came away :
So that one pious tear now must
Besprinkle either parent's dust,
And two great sorrows jointly run
And close into a larger one,
Or rather turn to joy, to see
The burial but the wedding be.

R. FLETCHER

AN EPITAPH

ON HIS DECEASED FRIEND.

HERE LIES the ruin'd Cabinet
   Of a rich Soul more highly set :
The dross and refuse of a Mind
Too glorious to be here confined.
Earth for a while bespoke his stay,
Only to bait, and so away :
So that what here he doated on
Was merely accommodation.
Not that his active soul could be
At home but in eternity,
Yet, while he bless'd us with the rays
Of his short-continued days,
Each minute had its weight of worth,
Each pregnant hour some star brought forth.
So, while he travel'd here beneath,
He lived when others only breathe :
For not a sand of time slipp'd by
Without its action sweet as high.
So good, so peaceable, so bless'd,—
Angels alone can speak the rest.

RICHARD FLECKNOE

CHLORIS

CHLORIS ! if ere May be done
You but offer to be gone,
Flowers will wither, green will fade,
Nothing fresh nor gay be had.
Farewell pleasure ! farewell Spring !
Farewell every sweeter thing !
The Year will pine away and mourn,
And Winter instantly return.

But, if you vouchsafe to stay
Only till the end of May,
Take it upon Flora's word,
Never sweeter Spring was tow'rd,
Never was Favonian wind
More propitiously inclined,
Never was in heaven nor earth
Promised more profuser mirth.

Such sweet force your presence has
To bring a joy to every place ;
Such a virtue has your sight,
All are cheer'd and gladded by 't ;
Such a freshness as does bring
Along with it perpetual Spring ;
Such a gaiety the while,
As makes both heaven and earth to smile.

JOHN BULTEEL

SONG

I GRANT your eyes are far more bright
Than ever was unclouded light;
And that love in your charming voice
As much of reason finds for choice:
Yet if you hate when I adore,
To do the like I find much more.

A voice would move all but a stone
Without kind love shall find me one;
And eyes the brightest ever shined
On me have power but as they're kind:
You must, to throw down all defence,
As much my reason please as sense.

I clearly know, say what you will,
To read my heart you want the skill;
And of this 'tis a pregnant sign,
Since you see not these truths of mine:
Which if you did, you would despair,
Without you loved, to form one there.

PART II — AUTHORS UNKNOWN

POEMS

PART II

FROM TOTTEL'S MISCELLANY

THE MEAN ESTATE HAPPIEST

IF right be rackt and over-run,
  And power take part with open wrong,
If fear by force do yield too soon :
The lack is like to last too long.

If God for goods shall be unplaced,
If right for riches lose his shape,
If world for wisdom be embraced :
The guess is great much hurt may hap.

Among good things, I prove and find,
The quiet life doth most abound :
And sure to the contented mind
There is no riches may be found.

For riches hates to be content ;
Rule enemy is to quietness ;
Power is most part impatient,
And seldom likes to live in peace.

I heard a herdman once compare :
That quiet nights he had more slept,
And had more merry days to spare,
Than he which own'd the beasts he kept.

I would not have it thought hereby
The dolphin swim I mean to teach ;
Nor yet to learn the falcon fly :
I row not so far past my reach.

But as my part above the rest
Is well to wish and well to will,
So till my breath shall fail my breast
I will not cease to wish you still.

HE WISHETH DEATH
Upon consideration of the state of this life.

THE longer life, the more offence ;
   The more offence, the greater pain ;
The greater pain, the less defence ;
   The less defence, the lesser gain :
The loss of gain long ill doth try :
Wherefore come death, and let me die !

The shorter life, less count I find ;
   The less account, the sooner made ;
The count soon made, the merrier mind ;
   The merry mind doth thought evade :
Short life in truth this thing doth try :
Wherefore come death, and let me die !

Come, gentle death ! the ebb of care ;
   The ebb of care, the flood of life ;

The flood of life, the joyful fare ;
   The joyful fare, the end of strife :
The end of strife, that thing wish I :
Wherefore come death, and let me die !

LOVE'S DISDAINER

The lover that once disdained Love is now subject,
being caught in his snare.

TO this my song give ear who list,
   And mine intent judge as you will !
The time is come that I have miss'd
   The thing whereon I hopèd still ;
And from the top of all my trust
Mishap hath thrown me in the dust.

The time hath been, and that of late,
   My heart (and I) might leap at large,
And was not shut within the gate
   Of love's desire ; nor took no charge
Of any thing that did pertain
As touching love in any pain :

My thought was free, my heart was light ;
   I marked not who lost, who saught :
I play'd by day, I slept by night ;
   I forcèd not who wept, who laught :
My thought from all such things was free,
And I myself at liberty.

I took no heed to taunts nor toys,
   As lief to see them frown as smile ;

Where fortune laught I scorn'd their joys,
   I found their frauds and every wile :
And to myself ofttimes I smiled
To see how love had them beguiled.

Thus in the net of my conceit
   I masked still among the sort
Of such as fed upon the bait
   That Cupid laid for his disport ;
And ever as I saw them caught
I them beheld and thereat laught.

Till at the length when Cupid spied
   My scornful will, and spiteful use,
And how I past not who was tied
   So that myself might still live loose,
He set himself to lie in wait :
And in my way he threw a bait.

Such one as Nature never made,
   I dare well say, save she alone :
Such one she was as would invade
   A heart more hard than marble stone :
Such one she is, I know it right,—
Her Nature made to show her might.

Then as a man even in a maze,
   Whose use of reason is away,
So I began to stare and gaze ;
   And suddenly, without delay,
Or ever I had wit to look,
I swallow'd up both bait and hook.

Which daily grieves me more and more
 By sundry sorts of careful woe ;
And none alive may salve the sore
 But only she that hurt me so :
In whom my life doth now consist,
To save or slay me as she list.

But seeing now that I am caught
 And bound so fast I can not flee,
Be ye by mine ensample taught,
 That in your fancies feel you free !
Despise not them that lovers are !
Lest you be caught within his snare.

WHERE GOOD WILL IS
SOME PROOF WILL APPEAR

IT is no fire that gives no heat,
 Though it appear never so hot ;
And they that run and can not sweat
 Are very lean and dry, God wot.

A perfect leech applieth his wits
 To gather herbs of all degrees ;
And fevers with their fervent fits
 Be curèd with their contraries.

New wine will search to find a vent,
 Although the cask be never so strong ;
And wit will walk when will is bent,
 Although the way be never so long.

The rabbits run under the rocks ;
 The snails do climb the highest towers ;

Gunpowder cleaves the sturdy blocks ;
    A fervent will all thing devours.

When wit with will, and diligent,
    Apply themselves and match as mates,
There can no want of resident
    From force defend the castle gates.

Forgetfulness makes little haste ;
    And sloth delights to lie full soft ;
That telleth the deaf, his tale doth waste ;
    And is full dry, that craves full oft.

PROMISE OF A CONSTANT LOVER

AS laurel leaves that cease not to be green,
    From parching sun, nor yet from winter's threat,
As harden'd oak that fear'th no sword so keen,
As flint for tool in twain that will not fret,—
As fast as rock or pillar surely set,—
So fast am I to you, and aye have been,
Assuredly whom I can not forget,
For joy, for pain, for torment, nor for tene,
For loss, for gain, for frowning, nor for let :
But ever one,— yea ! both in calm and blast,—
Your faithful friend, and will be to my last.

EACH THING HURT OF ITSELF

WHY fearest thou thy outward foe,
    When thou thyself thy harm dost feed?
Of grief, or hurt, of pain, or woe,
    Within each thing is sown a seed.

So fine was never yet the cloth,
    No smith so hard his iron did beat,
But the one consumèd was with moth,
    The other with canker all to fret.

The knotty oak and wainscoat old
    Within doth eat the silly worm :
Even so a mind in envy roll'd
    Always within itself doth burn.

Thus every thing that Nature wrought
    Within itself his hurt doth bear :
No outward harm need to be sought
    Whose enemies be within so near.

OF A ROSEMARY-BRANCH SENT

SUCH green to me as you have sent,
    Such green to you I send again :
A flowering heart that will not faint
    For dread of hope or loss of gain :
A steadfast thought all wholly bent
    So that he may your grace obtain,
As you by proof have always seen,
To live your own, and always green.

OF THE CHOICE OF A WIFE

THE flickering fame that flieth from ear to ear,
  And aye her strength increaseth with her flight,
Gives first the cause why men delight to hear
  Of those whom she doth note for beauty bright :
And with this fame that flieth on so fast
Fancy doth hie when reason makes no haste.

And yet, not so content, they wish to espy
  And thereby know if fame have said aright :
More trusting to the trial of their eye
  Than to the bruit that goes of any wight :
Wise in that point that lightly will not leave,
Unwise to seek that may them after grieve.

Who knoweth not how sight may love allure
  And kindle in the heart a hot desire,
The eye to work that fame could not procure :
  Of greater cause there cometh hotter fire :
For, ere he weet, himself he feeleth warm,
The fame and eye the causers of his harm.

Let fame not make her known whom I shall know,
  Nor yet mine eye, therein to be my guide :
Sufficeth me that virtue in her grow
  Whose simple life her father's walls do hide.
Content with this, I leave the rest to go :
And in such choice shall stand my wealth and woe.

OTHERS PREFERRED

SOME men would think of right to have
    For their true meaning some reward :
But while that I do cry and crave,
    I see that other be preferr'd.
    I gape for that I am debarr'd ;
I fare as doth the hound at hatch :
The worse I speed, the longer watch.

My wasteful will is tried by trust,
    My fond fancy is mine abuse ;
For that I would refrain my lust,—
    For mine avail I can not choose :
    A will, and yet no power to use ;
A will,— no will by reason just,
Since my will is at others' must.

They eat the honey, I hold the hive ;
    I sow the seed, they reap the corn ;
I waste, they win ; I draw, they drive ;
    Theirs is the thank, mine is the scorn ;
    I seek, they speed, in waste my wind is worn ;
I gape, they get, and greedily I snatch.
    Till worse I speed, the longer watch.

I fast, they feed ; they drink, I thirst ;
    They laugh, I wail ; they joy, I mourn ;
They gain, I lose, I have the worst ;
    They whole, I sick ; they cold, I burn ;
They leap, I iie ; they sleep, I toss and turn ;

I would, they may ; I crave, they have at will :
That helpeth them (lo ! cruelty) doth me kill.

NO JOY HAVE I

NO JOY HAVE I, but live in heaviness :
  My Dame of price bereft by Fortune's cruelness,
My hap is turned to unhappiness :
    Unhappy I am unless I find relesse.

My pastime past, my youth-like years are gone,
My months of mirth, my glistering days of gladsomeness,
  My times of triumph turned into moan :
    Unhappy I am unless I find relesse.

My wonted wind to chaunt my cheerful chance
Doth sigh that song sometime the ballad of my lesse ;
  My sobs my sore and sorrow do advance :
    Unhappy I am unless I find relesse.

I mourn my mirth for grief that it is gone,
I mourn my mirth whereof my musing mindfulness
  Is ground of greater grief that grows thereon :
    Unhappy I am unless I find relesse.

No joy have I : for Fortune frowardly
Hath bent her brows, hath put her hand to cruelness,
  Hath wrest my Dame, constrained me to cry —
    Unhappy I am unless I find relesse.

OF THE GOLDEN MEAN

THE wisest way thy boat in wave and wind to guie
Is neither still the trade of middle stream to try
Ne, warily shunning wreck by weather, aye too nigh
　　　To press upon the perilous shore.

Both cleanly flees he filth, ne wonnes a wretched wight
In carlish coat, and careful court (aye thrall to spite)
With port of proud estate he leaves, who doth delight
　　　Of golden mean to hold the lore.

Storms rifest rend the sturdy stout pine-apple tree :
Of lofty ruing towers the falls the feller be ;
Most fierce doth lightning light where farthest we do see
　　　The hills, the valley to forsake.

Well furnish'd breast to bide each chance's changeful cheer
In woe hath cheerful hope, in weal hath warefull fear :
One self Jove winter makes with loathful looks appear
　　　That can by course the same aslake.

What if into mishap the case now casten be,
It forceth not such form of luck to last to thee :
Not alway bent is Phœbus' bow ; his harp and he
　　　Ceased silver sound sometime doth raise.

In hardest hap use help of hardy hopeful heart ;
Seem bold, to bear the brunt of fortune overthwart ;
Eke wisely, when fore-wind to full breathes on thy part,
　　　'Suage swelling sail, and doubt decays !

THE PRAISE OF A TRUE FRIEND

WHOSO that wisely weighs the profit and the price
  Of things wherein delight by worth is wont to rise,
Shall find no jewel is so rich ne yet so rare
That with the friendly heart in value may compare.

What other wealth to man by fortune may befall,
But Fortune's changèd cheer may reave a man of all?
A friend no wrack of wealth, no cruel cause of woe,
Can cause his friendly faith unfriendly to forego.

If Fortune friendly fawn, and lend thee wealthy store,
Thy friend's conjoined joy doth make thy joy the more ;
If frowardly she frown, and drive thee to distress,
His aid relieves thy ruth and makes thy sorrow less.

Thus Fortune's pleasant fruits by friends increasèd be ;
The bitter, sharp, and sour, by friends allay'd to thee :
That when thou dost rejoice, then doubled is thy joy ;
And eke in cause of care the less is thy annoy.

Aloft if thou dost live, as one appointed here
A stately part on stage of worldly state to bear,
Thy friend, as only free from fraud, will thee advise
To rest within the rule of mean, as do the wise.

He seeketh to foresee the peril of thy fall ;
He findeth out thy faults, and warns thee of them all ;
Thee, not thy luck, he loves : whatever be thy case,
He is thy faithful friend, and thee he doth embrace.

If churlish cheer of chance have thrown thee into thrall,
And that thy need ask aid for to relieve thy fall,
In him thou secret trust assurèd art to have,
And succour, not to seek, before that thou can crave.

Thus is thy friend to thee the comfort of thy pain,
The stayer of thy state, the doubler of thy gain;
In wealth and woe thy friend, an other self to thee:
Such man to man a God, the proverb saith to be.

As wealth will bring thee friends in lowering woe to prove,
So woe shall yield thee friends in laughing wealth to love:
With wisdom choose thy friend;—with virtue him retain!
Let virtue be the ground! So shall it not be vain.

FROM THE PARADISE OF DAINTY DEVICES

LIFE'S STAY

Man's flitting life finds surest stay
Where sacred Virtue beareth sway.

THE sturdy rock, for all his strength,
  By raging seas is rent in twain;
The marble stone is pierced at length
  With little drops of drizzling rain;
The ox doth yield unto the yoke;
The steel obeys the hammer-stroke;

The stately stag, that seems so stout,
    By yelping hounds at bay is set ;
The swiftest bird that flies about
    Is caught at length in fowler's net ;
The greatest fish in deepest brook
Is soon deceived with subtle hook ;

Yea, man himself, unto whose will
    All things are bounden to obey,
For all his wit and worthy skill
    Doth fade at length and fall away.
There is no thing but Time doth waste ;
The heavens, the earth, consume at last.

But Virtue sits, triùmphing still,
    Upon the throne of glorious fame :
Though spiteful Death man's body kill,
    Yet hurts he not his virtuous name.
By life or death, whatso betides,
The state of Virtue never slides.

THE LOST FRIEND

WHY should I longer long to live
    In this disease of fantasy?
Since Fortune doth not cease to give
    Things to my mind most contrary ;
And at my joys doth lour and frown,
Till she hath turn'd them upside down.

A friend I had, to me most dear,
    And of long time, faithful and just,—

There was no one my heart so near,
  Nor one in whom I had more trust,—
Whom now of late, without cause why,
Fortune hath made my enemy.

The grass, methinks, should grow in sky,
  The stars unto the earth cleave fast,
The water-stream should pass awry,
  The winds should leave their strength of blast,
The sun and moon by one assent
Should both forsake the firmament,

The fish in air should fly with fin,
  The fowls in flood should bring forth fry,
All things, methinks, should first begin
  To take their course unnaturally,
Afore my friend should alter so,
Without a cause to be my foe.

But such is Fortune's hate, I say,
  Such is her will on me to wreak,
Such spite she hath at me alway,
  And ceaseth not my heart to break :
With such despite of cruelty,
Wherefore then longer live should I ?

MAY

WHEN MAY is in his prime,
  Then may each heart rejoice ;
When May bedecks each branch with green,
  Each bird strains forth his voice.

The lively sap creeps up
  Into the blooming thorn ;
The flowers, which cold in prison kept,
  Now laugh the frost to scorn.

All Nature's imps triùmph
  Whiles joyful May doth last ;
When May is gone, of all the year
  The pleasant time is past.

May makes the cheerful hue ;
  May breeds and brings new blood ;
May marcheth throughout every limb ;
  May makes the merry mood.

May pricketh tender hearts
  Their warbling notes to tune ;—
Full strange it is, yet some, we see,
  Do make their May in June.

Thus things are strangely wrought
  Whiles joyful May doth last :
Take May in time ! when May is gone,
  The pleasant time is past.

All ye that live on earth,
　And have your May at will,
Rejoice in May, as I do now,
　And use your May with skill !

Use May while that you may,
　For May hath but his time !
When all the fruit is gone it is
　Too late the tree to climb.

Your liking and your lust
　Is fresh whiles May doth last :
When May is gone, of all the year
　The pleasant time is past.

FROM BYRD'S SET SONGS

RIGHT CAREFULNESS

CARE for thy soul as thing of greatest price,
　Made to the end to taste of power divine,
Devoid of guilt, abhorring sin and vice,
　Apt by God's grace to virtue to incline !
Care for it so that by thy reckless train
It be not brought to taste eternal pain !

Care for thy corpse, but chiefly for soul's sake !
Cut off excess ! sustaining food is best.

To vanquish pride, but comely clothing take !
   Seek after skill ! deep ignorance detest !
Care so (I say) the flesh to feed and clothe,
That thou harm not thy soul and body both !

Care for the world, to do thy body right !
   Rack not thy wit to win by wicked ways !
Seek not to oppress the weak by wrongful might !
   To pay thy due do banish all delays !
Care to dispend according to thy store ;
And in like sort be mindful of the poor !

Care for thy soul, as for thy chiefest stay !
   Care for the body, for the soul's avail !
Care for the world, for body's help alway !
   Care yet but so as virtue may prevail !
Care in such sort that thou beware of this —
Care keep thee not from heaven and heavenly bliss !

LOVE'S ARROWS

The golden and leaden arrows of Love

FROM Citheron the warlike Boy is fled,
   And smiling sits upon a Virgin's lap,—
   Thereby to train poor misers to the trap,
Whom Beauty draws with fancy to be fed :
And when Desire with eager looks is led,
     Then from her eyes
     The arrow flies,
Feather'd with flame, arm'd with a golden head.

Her careless thoughts are freèd of that flame
   Wherewith her thralls are scorched to the heart :
   If Love would so, would God the enchanting dart
Might once return and burn from whence it came !
Not to deface of Beauty's work the frame,
         But by rebound
         It might be found
What secret smart I suffer by the same.

If Love be just, then just is my desire ;
   And if unjust, why is he call'd a God?
   O god, O god, O Just ! reserve thy rod
To chasten those that from thy laws retire !
But choose aright (good Love ! I thee require),
         The golden head,
         Not that of lead !
Her heart is frost and must dissolve by fire.

LOVE'S QUALITIES

IS LOVE a boy,— what means he then to strike?
   Or is he blind,— why will he be a guide?
   Is he a man,— why doth he hurt his like?
   Is he a god,— why doth he men deride?
   No one of these, but one compact of all :
   A wilful boy, a man still dealing blows,
   Of purpose blind to lead men to their thrall,
   A god that rules unruly — God, he knows.

Boy ! pity me that am a child again ;
   Blind, be no more my guide to make me stray :

Man ! use thy might to force away my pain ;
God ! do me good and lead me to my way ;
And if thou beest a power to me unknown,
Power of my life ! let here thy grace be shown.

CUPID'S DELIVERANCE

UPON a summer's day Love went to swim,
  And cast himself into a sea of tears ;
The clouds call'd in their light, and heaven wax'd dim,
And sighs did raise a tempest, causing fears.
The naked boy could not so wield his arms
But that the waves were masters of his might,
And threaten'd him to work far greater harms
If he devisèd not to escape by flight.

Then for a boat his quiver stood in stead,
His bow unbent did serve him for a mast,
Whereby to sail his cloth of vayle he spread.
His shafts for oars on either board he cast :
From shipwreck safe this wag got thus to shore,
And sware to bathe in lovers' tears no more.

THE HERD-MAN'S HAPPY LIFE

WHAT pleasure have great princes
  More dainty to their choice
Than herd-men wild who, careless,
  In quiet life rejoice
And, fickle Fortune scorning,
  Sing sweet in summer morning?

Their dealings, plain and rightful,
   Are void of all deceit;
They never know how spiteful
   It is to kneel and wait
On favourite presumptuous
Whose pride is vain and sumptuous.

All day their flocks each tendeth,
   At night they take their rest:
More quiet than who sendeth
   His ship into the East,
Where gold and pearl are plenty,
But getting very dainty.

For lawyers and their pleading,
   They esteem it not a straw;
They think that honest meaning
   Is of itself a law:
Where conscience judgeth plainly
They spend no money vainly.

O, happy who thus liveth,
   Not caring much for gold,
With clothing that sufficeth
   To keep him from the cold:
Though poor and plain his diet,
Yet merry it is and quiet.

PHILON THE SHEPHERD
HIS SONG

WHILE that the sun with his beams hot
  Scorched the fruits in vale and mountain,
Philon, the shepherd, late forgot
  Sitting beside a crystal fountain,
    In shadow of a green oak tree,
    Upon his pipe this song play'd he :
Adieu, Love ! adieu, Love ! untrue Love !
Untrue Love, untrue Love ! adieu, Love !
Your mind is light, soon lost for a new love.

So long as I was in your sight,
  I was your heart, your soul, your treasure ;
And evermore you sobb'd and sigh'd,
  Burning in flames beyond all measure.
    Three days endured your love for me,
    And it was lost in other three.
Adieu, Love ! adieu, Love ! untrue Love !
Untrue Love, untrue Love ! adieu, Love !
Your mind is light, soon lost for a new love.

Another shepherd you did see,
  To whom your heart was soon enchainèd ;
Full soon your love was leapt from me,
  Full soon my place he had obtainèd :
    Soon came a third your love to win ;
    And we were out, and he was in.
Adieu, Love ! adieu, Love ! untrue Love !
Untrue Love ! untrue Love ! adieu, Love !
Your mind is light, soon lost for a new love.

Sure, you have made me passing glad
   That you your mind so soon removèd,
Before that I the leisure had
   To choose you for my best-belovèd :
     For all my love was past and done
     Two days before it was begun.
Adieu, Love ! adieu, Love ! untrue Love !
Untrue Love, untrue Love ! adièu, Love !
Your mind is light, soon lost for a new love.

BROWN IS MY LOVE

BROWN is my Love, but graceful :
   And each renowned whiteness
Match'd with her lovely brown loseth its brightness.

   Fair is my Love, but scornful :
   Yet have I seen despisèd
White dainty lilies, and sad flowers well prizèd.

CYNTHIA

CYNTHIA, thy song and chaunting
   So strange a flame in gentle hearts awaketh
That every cold desire wanton Love maketh
    Sounds to thy praise and vaunting,
Of Syrens most commended
That with delightful tunes for praise contended !
    For, when thou sweetly soundest,
    Thou neither kill'st nor woundest,
    But dost revive a number
Of bodies buried in perpetual slumber.

THE ANATOMY OF LOVE

NOW what is love? I pray thee tell.
   It is that fountain and that well
Where pleasure and repentance dwell :
It is perhaps that sauncing bell
That tolls all in to heaven or hell :
And this is love, as I hear tell.

Yet, what is love? I pray thee say.
It is a work on holiday :
It is December match'd with May :
When lusty bloods, in fresh array,
Hear ten months after of the play :
And this is love, as I hear say.

Yet, what is love? I pray thee sain.
It is a sunshine mix'd with rain :
It is a toothache, or like pain :
It is a game where none doth gain :
The lass saith Oh ! and would full fain :
And this is love, as I hear sain.

Yet, what is love? I pray thee say.
It is a Yea, it is a Nay :
A pretty kind of sporting fray :
It is a thing will soon away :
Then take the vantage while you may !
And this is love, as I hear say.

Yet, what is love? I pray thee show.
A thing that creeps, it can not go :
A prize that passeth to and fro :
A thing for me, a thing for mo :
And he that proves must find it so :
And this is love, sweet friend ! I trow.

TO NIGHT

O NIGHT ! O jealous Night ! repugnant to my
measures ;
O Night so long desired, yet cross to my content !
There 's none but only thou that can perform my
pleasures,
Yet none but only thou that hindereth my intent.

Thy beams, thy spiteful beams, thy lamps that burn
too brightly,
Discover all my trains and naked lay my drifts :
That night by night I hope, yet fails my purpose nightly,
Thy envious glaring gleam defeateth so my shifts.

Sweet Night ! withhold thy beams, withhold them till
to-morrow,
Whose joys in lack so long a hell of torment breeds ;
Sweet Night, sweet gentle Night ! do not prolong my
sorrow !
Desire is guide to me, and love no loadstar needs.

Let sailors gaze on stars and moon so freshly shining ;
Let them that miss the way be guided by the light :
I know my Lady's bower, there needs no more divining,

Affection sees in dark, and love hath eyes by night.

Dame Cynthia ! couch awhile, hold in thy horns from
                                              shining,
And glad not louring Night with thy too glorious rays ;
But be she dim and dark, tempestuous and repining,
That in her spite my sport may work thy endless praise.

And when my will is wrought, then Cynthia ! shine,
                                              good lady !
All other nights and days, in honour of that night,
That happy heavenly night, that night so dark and shady,
Wherein my love had eyes that lighted my delight !

SET ME WHERE PHŒBUS

SET ME where Phœbus' heat the flowers slayeth,
    Or where continual snow withstands his forces ;
Set me where he his temperate rays displayeth,
    Or where he comes, or where he never courses !

Set me in Fortune's grace, or else dischargèd ;
    In sweet and pleasant air, or dark and glooming ;
Where days and nights are lesser or enlargèd ;
    In years of strength, in failing age, or blooming !

Set me in heaven, or earth, or in the centre ;
    Low in a vale, or on a mountain placèd ;
Set me to danger, peril, or adventure,
    Gracèd by fame, or infamy disgracèd !

Set me to these, or any other trial
    Except my Mistress' anger and denial.

THE LOVER'S DESPAIR

FLOW FORTH, abundant tears !
   Bedew this doleful face ;
Disorder now thy hairs,
   That livest in such disgrace !

Ah ! death exceedeth far
   This life which I endure,
That still keeps me in war,
   Who no peace can procure.

I love whom I should hate ;
   She flies, I follow fast :
Such is my bitter state,
   I wish no life to last.

Alas ! affection strong
   To whom I must obey
My reason so doth wrong
   As it can bear no sway.

My field of flint I find,
   My harvest vain desire :
For he that sowed wind
   Now reapeth storm for hire.

Alas ! like flowers of spine
   Thy graces rosy be :

I prick these hands of mine,
　For haste to gather thee.

But now shall sorrow slake ;
　I yield to mortal strife :
To die thus for thy sake
　Shall honour all my life.

LOVE AND SORROW

L OVE is a spirit high presuming,
　That falleth oft ere he sit fast ;
Care is a sorrow long consuming,
　Which yet doth kill the heart at last ;
Death is a wrong to life and love :
And I the pains of all must prove.

Words are but trifles in regarding,
　And pass away as puffs of wind ;
Deeds are too long in their rewarding,
　And out of sight are out of mind :
And those so little favour feed,
As finds no fruit in word or deed.

Truth is a thought too long in trial,
　And, known, but coldly entertain'd ;
Love is too long in his denial,
　And in the end but hardly gain'd :
And in the gain the sweet so small,
That I must taste the sour of all.

But O ! the death too long enduring,
Where nothing can my pain appease ;

And O ! the cure so long in curing,
  Where patient hurt hath never ease :
And O ! that ever love should know
The ground whereof a grief doth grow.

But, heavens ! heal me from this hell ;
Or let me die, and I am well.

SERENADE

COME AWAY ! come, sweet Love !
  The golden morning breaks :
All the earth, all the air,
  Of love and pleasure speaks.
Teach thine arms then to embrace,
  And sweet rosy lips to kiss,
And mix our souls in mutual bliss :
Eyes were made for beauty's grace,
Viewing, ruing love-long pain
Procured by beauty's rude disdain.

Come away ! come, sweet Love !
  The golden morning wastes
While the sun from his sphere
  His fiery arrows casts :
Making all the shadows fly,
  Playing, staying in the grove
To entertain the stealth of love.
Thither, sweet Love ! let us hie,
Flying, dying in desire,
Wing'd with sweet hopes and heavenly fire.

Come away ! come, sweet Love !
　　Do not in vain adorn
Beauty's grace, that should rise
　　Like to the naked Morn.
Lilies on the river side
And fair Cyprian flowers new-blown
　　Desire no beauties but their own :
Ornament is nurse of pride.
Pleasure measures love's delight :
Haste then, sweet Love ! our wished flight.

CONSTANCY

DEAR ! if you change, I 'll never choose again ;
　　Sweet ! if you shrink, I 'll never think of love ;
Fair ! if you fail, I 'll judge all beauty vain ;
Wise ! if too weak, more wits I 'll never prove.
Dear ! Sweet ! Fair ! Wise ! change, shrink not,
　　　　　　　　　　　　nor be weak :
And, on my faith, my faith shall never break.

Earth with her flowers shall sooner heaven adorn ;
Heaven her bright stars through earth's dim globe
　　　　　　　　　　　　shall move ;
Fire heat shall lose, and frosts of flames be born ;
Air, made to shine, as black as hell shall prove :
Earth, heaven, fire, air, the world transform'd shall
　　　　　　　　　　　　view,
Ere I prove false to faith or strange to you.

TO CYNTHIA

MY THOUGHTS are wing'd with hope, my
     hopes with love :
 Mount, love ! unto the Moon in clearest night ;
And say, as she doth in the heavens move,
 In earth so wanes and waxes my delight.
And whisper this, but softly, in her ears,—
Hope oft doth hang the head, and trust shed tears.

And you, my thoughts ! that some mistrust do carry,
 If for mistrust my Mistress do you blame,
Say, though you alter, yet you do not vary,
 As she doth change and yet remain the same :
Distrust doth enter hearts, but not infect,
And love is sweetest season'd with suspect.

If she for this with clouds do mask her eyes,
 And make the heavens dark with her disdain,
With windy sighs disperse them in the skies,
 Or with thy tears dissolve them into rain !
Thoughts, hopes, and love, return to me no more
Till Cynthia shine as she hath done before !

LOVE'S MESSENGERS

GO, crystal tears ! like to the morning showers,
 And sweetly weep into my Lady's breast ;
 And, as the dews revive the drooping flowers,
  So let your drops of pity be address'd
 To quicken up the thoughts of my desart,
 Which sleep too sound whilst I from her depart.

Haste, restless sighs ! and let your burning breath
    Dissolve the ice of her indùrate heart,
Whose frozen rigour, like forgetful death,
    Feels never any touch of my desart :
Yet sighs and tears to her I sacrifice,
Both from a spotless heart and patient eyes.

WEEP YOU NO MORE

WEEP YOU NO MORE, sad fountains !
    What need you flow so fast ?
Look how the snowy mountains
    Heaven's sun doth gently waste !
But my sun's heavenly eyes
    View not your weeping,
    That now lies sleeping
Softly, now softly lies,
        Sleeping.

Sleep is a reconciling,
    A rest that peace begets :
Doth not the sun rise smiling
    When fair at even he sets ?
Rest you then, rest, sad eyes !
    Melt not in weeping !
    While she lies sleeping
Softly, now softly lies,
        Sleeping.

WHITE AS LILIES

WHITE AS LILIES was her face :
          When She smilèd
          She beguilèd,
Quiting faith with foul disgrace.
Virtue's service thus neglećted
Heart with sorrows hath infećted.

When I swore my heart her own,
          She disdained ;
          I complained,
Yet She left me overthrown :
Careless of my bitter grieving,
Ruthless, bent to no relieving.

Vows and oaths and faith assurèd,
          Constant ever,
          Changing never,—
Yet She could not be procurèd
To believe my pains exceeding
From her scant respećt proceeding.

O that love should have the art,
          By surmises,
          And disguises,
To destroy a faithful heart ;
Or that wanton-looking women
Should regard their friends as foemen !

All in vain is ladies' love,—
          Quickly choosèd,

Shortly loosèd :
For their pride is to remove.
Out, alas ! their looks first won us,
And their pride hath straight undone us.

To thyself, the Sweetest Fair !
    Thou hast wounded,
    And confounded
Changeless faith with foul despair ;
And my service hast envièd,
And my succours hast denièd.

By thine error thou hast lost
    Heart unfeigned,
    Truth unstained,
And the swain that lovèd most,
More assured in love than many,
More despised in love than any.

For my heart, though set at nought,
    Since you will it,
    Spoil and kill it !
I will never change my thought :
But grieve that beauty e'er was born
Thus to answer love with scorn.

EYES AND HEARTS

NOW CEASE, my wandering eyes !
　　Strange beauties to admire ;
In change least comfort lies,
　　Long joys yield long desire.
　　One faith, one love,
Makes our frail life eternal sweetness prove ;
　　New hopes, new joys,
Are still with sore declining unto deep annoys.

One man hath but one soul,
　　Which art can not divide :
If all must love one whole,
　　Two loves must be denied. ?
　　One soul, one love,
By faith and merit knit, can not remove ;
　　Distracted sprights
Are ever changing and hapless in their delights.

Nature two eyes hath given,
　　All beauty to impart,
As well in earth as heaven :
　　But she hath given one heart
　　That, though we see
Ten thousand beauties, yet in us should be
　　One stedfast love,—
Because our hearts stand fix'd, although our eyes
　　　　　　　　do move.

FALSE ASTRONOMY

WHAT poor astronomers are they
    Take women's eyes for stars,
And set their thoughts in battle array
    To fight such idle wars,
When in the end they shall approve
'Tis but a jest drawn out of love.

And love itself is but a jest,
    Devised by idle heads
To catch young Fancies in the nest,
    And lay them in fools' beds :
That, being hatch'd in Beauty's eyes,
They may be fledged ere they be wise.

But yet it is a sport to see
    How Wit will run on wheels,
While Wit can not persuaded be
    With that which Wisdom feels :
That woman's eyes and stars are odd ;
And Love is but a feigned god.

But such as will run mad with will,—
    I can not clear their sight,
But leave them to their study still,
    To look where is no light :
Till time too late we make them try
They study false astronomy.

THE HERMIT'S SONG

FROM fame's desire, from love's delight retired,
  In these sad groves an hermit's life I lead ;
And those false pleasures which I once admired
  With sad remembrance of my fall I dread.
To birds, to trees, to earth, impart I this :
For She less secret and as senseless is.

Experience, which repentance only brings,
  Doth bid me now my heart from love estrange :
Love is disdain'd when it doth look at kings,
  And love low placèd base and apt to change.
Their power doth take from him his liberty ;
Her want of worth makes him in cradle die.

You men that give false worship unto Love
  And seek that which you never shall obtain,
The endless work of Sisiphus you prove,
  Whose end is this — to know you strive in vain.
Hope and Desire, which now your idols be,
You needs must lose, and feel despair with me.

You woods ! in you the fairest nymphs have walk'd,
  Nymphs at whose sight all hearts did yield to love ;
You woods ! in whom dear lovers oft have talk'd :
  How do you now a place of mourning prove !
Wanstead ! my Mistress saith this is the doom.
Thou art love's child-bed, nursery, and tomb.

LOVE AND FORTUNE

FACTION, that ever dwells in Court, where wit
    excels,
        Hath set defiance :
Fortune and Love have sworn that they were never
    born
        Of one alliance.

Cupid, which doth aspire to be God of desire,
        Swears he gives laws ;
That where his arrows hit some joy, some sorrow it :
        Fortune no cause.

Fortune swears weakest hearts (the books of Cupid's
    arts)
        Turn'd with her wheel
Senseless themselves shall prove ; venter hath place
    in love,—
        Ask them that feel !

This discord, it begot atheists that honour not :
        Nature thought good
Fortune should ever dwell in Court, where wits excel,
        Love keep the wood.

So to the wood went I, with Love to live and die,
        Fortune's Forlorn :
Experience of my youth made me think humble Truth
        In desert born.

My Saint I keep to me,—and Joan herself is she,
        Joan fair and true :
Joan, she doth only move passion of love with love.
        Fortune ! adieu !
                        FINIS, E. O.

HIS LADY'S GRIEF

I SAW my Lady weep,
    And Sorrow proud to be advancèd so
In those fair eyes where all perfections keep.
        Her face was full of woe :
But such a woe, believe ! as wins more hearts
Than Mirth can do with her enticing parts.

Sorrow was there made fair,
    And passion wise, tears a delightful thing,
Silence beyond all speech a wisdom rare ;
        She made her sighs to sing,
And all things with so sweet a sadness move
As made my heart at once both grieve and love.

O, Fairer than aught else
The world can show, leave off in time to grieve !
Enough ! enough ! your joyful look excels :
        Tears kill the heart, believe !
O strive not to be excellent in woe,
Which only breeds your beauty's overthrow !

SONG OF HOPE

DIE NOT before thy day, poor man condemn'd !
But lift thy low looks from the humble earth :
Kiss not Despair, nor see sweet Hope contemn'd ;
    The hag hath no delight, but moan for mirth.
        O, fie ! poor fondling, fie ! be willing
        To preserve thyself from killing !
        Hope, thy keeper, glad to free thee,
        Bids thee go, and will not see thee.
        Hie thee quickly from thy wrong !—
        So she ends her willing song.

WOEFUL HEART

WOEFUL HEART, with grief oppressed !
Since my fortunes most distressed
    From my joys have me removèd,
Follow those sweet eyes adorèd,
Those sweet eyes wherein are storèd
    All my pleasures best belovèd !

Fly my breast — leave me forsaken —
Wherein Grief his seat hath taken,
    All his arrows through me darting !
Thou mayst live by her sun-shining :
I shall suffer no more pining
    By thy loss than by her parting.

HIS MISTRESS' BEAUTY

I MUST complain, yet do enjoy my Love :
    She is too fair, too rich in beauty's parts.
Thence is my grief : for Nature, while she strove
    With all her graces and divinest arts
To form her too too beautiful of hue,
She had no leisure left to make her true.

Should I aggrieved then wish she were less fair?
    That were repugnant to my own desires.
She is admired ; new suitors still repair
    That kindle daily Love's forgetful fires.
Rest, jealous thoughts ! and thus resolve at last :
She hath more beauty than becomes the chaste.

LOVE AND FOLLY

BEHOLD a wonder here !
    Love hath received his sight :
Which many hundred year
    Hath not beheld the light.

Such beams infusèd be
    By Cynthia in his eyes,
As first have made him see,
    And then have made him wise.

Love now no more will weep
    For them that laugh the while,
Nor wake for them that sleep,
    Nor sigh for them that smile.

So powerful is the Beauty
   That Love doth now behold,
As Love is turn'd to Duty,
   That 's neither blind nor bold.

Thus Beauty shows her might
   To be of double kind :
In giving Love his sight,
   And striking Folly blind.

THE PEDLAR'S SONG

FINE knacks for ladies, cheap, choice, brave, and new,
Good pennyworths,— but money can not move :
I keep a fair but for the Fair to view,—
   A beggar may be liberal in love.
Though all my wares be trash, the heart is true :
                  The heart is true.

Great gifts are guiles and look for gifts again ;
   My trifles come as treasures from my mind :
It is a precious jewel,— to be plain :
   Sometimes in shells the orient pearls we find.—
Of others take a sheaf, of me a grain !
                  Of me a grain.

Within this pack are pins, points, laces, gloves,
   And divers toys fitting a country Fair ;
But my heart, wherein duty serves and loves —
   Turtles and twins, courts brood, a heavenly pair.
Happy the heart that thinks of no remove !
                  Of no remove.

DEFIANCE TO LOVE

SHOOT, FALSE LOVE! I care not:
   Spend thy shafts and spare not!   Fa la la!
I fear not, I, thy might,
And less I weigh thy spite;
All naked I unarm me,—
If thou canst, now shoot and harm me!
So lightly I esteem thee
As now a child I deem thee.

Fa la la la!

Long thy bow did fear me,
While thy pomp did blear me: Fa la la!
But now I do perceive
Thy art is to deceive;
And every simple lover
All thy falsehood can discover.
Then weep, Love! and be sorry,
For thou hast lost thy glory.

Fa la la la!

MY DAINTY DARLING

WHAT saith my Dainty Darling?
   Shall I now your love obtain?
Long time I sued for grace,
   And grace you granted me
"When time should serve and place."
   Can any fitter be?

This crystal running fountain
In his language saith — Come, love !
The birds, the trees, the fields,—
    Else none can us behold ;
This bank soft lying yields,
And saith — Nice fools ! be bold.
                Fa la la la !

FALSE CLARINDA

PHILISTUS' FAREWELL

CLARINDA false ! adieu ! thy love torments me :
Let Thirsis have thy heart, since he contents thee.
    O grief and bitter anguish !
    For thee I languish :
    Fain I, alas ! would hide it :
    O, but who can abide it ?
    Adieu, adieu, adieu then !
        Farewell !
Leave me ! my death now desiring,
Thou hast, lo ! thy requiring.—
So spake Philistus on his hook relying,
    And sweetly fell a-dying.

    Since my tears and lamenting,
    False Love ! bred thy contenting,
    Still thus to weep for ever
    These fountains shall persèver,
    Till my heart, grief brim-filled,
    Out, alas ! be distilled.—
    So spake he on his hook relying,
        And sweetly fell a-dying.

FALSE DORUS

IN dew of roses steeping
   Her lovely cheeks, Lycoris sat a-weeping :—
Ah, Dorus false ! thou hast my heart bereft me,
     And now, unkind, hast left me.
       Hear, alas, O hear me !
         Ay me, ay me,
     Can not my beauty move thee ?
        Pity then, pity me
        Because I love thee !
Ay me, thou scorn'st the more I pray thee ;
    And this thou dost to slay me.
Ah, do then, do, kill me and vaunt thee !
    Yet my ghost still shall haunt thee.

FROM WILBYE'S MADRIGALS

DAPHNE

I SANG sometimes my thoughts and fancies' pleasure.
  Where then I list, or time served best and leisure :
     While Daphne did invite me
   To supper once, and drank to me to spite me.
     I smiled, yet still did doubt her,
And drank where she had drunk before, to flout her.
     But O, while I did eye her,
Mine eyes drank love, my lips drank burning fire.

THE JEWEL

THERE is a jewel which no Indian mine can buy,
     No chemic art can counterfeit :
It makes men rich in greatest poverty,
Makes water wine, turns wooden cups to gold,
The homely whistle to sweet music's strain :
Seldom it comes, to few from heaven sent,
That much in little, all in nought,— Content.

LIPS AND ROSES

LADY! when I behold the roses sprouting,
    Which clad in damask mantles deck the arbours,
And then behold your lips where sweet love harbours,
    My eyes present me with a double doubting :
For, viewing both alike, hardly my mind supposes
Whether the roses be your lips or your lips be the roses.

COME, SHEPHERD SWAINS!

COME, shepherd swains that wont to hear me sing !
     Now sigh and groan !
Dead is my Love, my Hope, my Joy, my Spring :
     Dead, dead, and gone.
   O, She that was your summers' queen,
     Your days' delight,
  Is gone, and will no more be seen :
     O cruel spite !
Break all your pipes that wont to sound
     With pleasant cheer,

And cast yourselves upon the ground,
To wail my Dear !
Come, shepherd swains ! come, nymphs ! and all a-row,
To help me cry :
Dead is my Love ; and, seeing She is so,
Lo ! now I die.

LOVE ME NOT FOR COMELY GRACE

LOVE ME not for comely grace,
For my pleasing eye or face,
Nor for any outward part ;
No ! nor for my constant heart !
For these may fail, or turn to ill :
So thou and I shall sever.
Keep therefore a true woman's eye,
And love me well, yet know not why !
So hast thou the same reason still
To doat upon me ever.

SWEET NIGHT

DRAW on, sweet Night ! best friend unto those cares
That do arise from painful melancholy :
My life so ill through want of comfort fares,
That unto thee I consecrate it wholly.

Sweet Night ! draw on : my griefs, when they be told
To shades and darkness, find some ease from paining ;
And while thou all in silence dost infold,
I then shall have best time for my complaining.

FROM WEELKES' BALLETS AND MADRIGALS

THIRSIS

UPON A HILL the bonny boy,
   Sweet Thirsis, sweetly play'd,
And call'd his lambs their master's joy :
   And more he would have said,
But love, that gives the lover wings,
Withdrew his mind from other things.

His pipe and he could not agree,
   For Milla was his note :
The silly pipe could never get
   This lovely name by rote.
With that they both fell on a sound :
He fell asleep, his pipe to ground.

SPRING SONG

IN pride of May
   The fields are gay,
The birds do sweetly sing :
   So Nature would
   That all things should
With joy begin the Spring.

   Then, Lady dear !
   Do you appear
In beauty, like the Spring !
   I well dare say
   The birds that day
More cheerfully will sing.

HOLD OUT, MY HEART!

HOLD out, my heart ! with joy's delights accloy'd,
    Hold out, my heart ! and show it,
    That all the world may know it,
What sweet content thou lately hast enjoy'd.
    She that " Come, Dear ! " would say,
    Then laugh, and smile, and run away,
    And if I stay'd her would cry " Nay !
       Fie ! for shame ! fie ! "
My true love not regarding,
Hath given me at length his full rewarding :
    So that, unless I tell
      The joys that overfill me,
    My joys kept in — full well
      I know — will kill me.

FROM FARMER'S ENGLISH MADRIGALS

TIME NOT TO BE LOST

TAKE time while time doth last !
  Mark how fair fadeth fast !
Beware, beware if Envy reign !
Beware, take heed of proud disdain !
Hold fast now in thy youth,—
Now regard thy vowed truth,—
Lest when thou waxeth old
Friends fail and love grow cold !

THE COY MAIDEN'S CONSENT

O STAY, sweet Love ! see here the place of sporting ;
   These gentle flowers smile sweetly to invite us ;
And chirping birds are hitherwards resorting,
   Warbling their sweet notes only to delight us :
Then stay, dear Love ! for though thou run from me,
   Run ne'er so fast, yet I will follow thee.

I thought, my Love ! that I should overtake you :
Sweetheart ! sit down under this shadow'd tree ;
   And I will promise never to forsake you,
     So you will grant to me a lover's fee.
Whereat She smiled, and kindly to me said —
   " I never meant to live and die a maid."

FAIR PHILLIS

FAIR PHILLIS I saw sitting all alone,
   Feeding her flock near to the mountain side :
The shepherds knew not whither she was gone,
   But after her her Love, Amyntas, hied.
He wander'd up and down whilst she was missing :
When he found her, then they fell a-kissing.

FROM BATESON'S MADRIGALS

SISTER, AWAKE!

SISTER, AWAKE ! close not your eyes !
    The day its light discloses :
And the bright Morning doth arise
    Out of her bed of roses.

See ! the clear Sun, the world's bright eye,
    In at our window peeping !
Lo, how he blusheth to espy
    Us idle wenches sleeping.

Therefore awake ! make haste ! I say ;
    And let us, without staying,
All in our gowns of green so gay
    Into the park a-maying.

WHITHER SO FAST?

WHITHER so fast? Ah, see ! the kindly flowers
    Perfume the air, and all to make thee stay :
The climbing woodbine, clipping all these bowers,
    Clips thee likewise, for fear thou pass away :
    Fortune our friend, our foe will not gainsay.
      Stay but awhile ! Phœbe no tell-tale is :
      She her Endymion, I 'll my Phœbe kiss.

LOVE TILL DEATH

THERE IS a Lady, sweet and kind,—
Was never face so pleased my mind!
I did but see her passing by,
And yet I love her till I die.

Her gesture, motion, and her smiles,
Her wit, her voice, my heart beguiles:
Beguiles my heart, I know not why:
And yet I love her till I die.

Her free behaviour, winning looks,
Will make a lawyer burn his books:
I touch'd her not,— alas! not I:
And yet I love her till I die.

Had I her fast betwixt my arms,—
Judge, you that think such sports were harms!
Were 't any harm? No, no! fie, fie!
For I will love her till I die.

Should I remain confinèd there
So long as Phœbus in his sphere,
I to request, she to deny,
Yet would I love her till I die.

Cupid is winged, and doth range
Her country,— so my Love doth change:
But change the earth or change the sky,
Yet will I love her till I die.

A MISTRESS DESCRIBED

HOW shall I then describe my Love?
    When all men's skilful art
Is far inferior to her worth,
    To praise the unworthiest part.

She's chaste in looks, mild in her speech,
    In actions all discreet,
Of nature loving, pleasing most,
    In virtue all complete.

And for her voice a Philomel,
    Her lips may all lips scorn;
No sun more clear than is her eye,
    In brightest summer morn.

A mind wherein all virtues rest
    And take delight to be,
And where all virtues graft themselves
    In that most fruitful tree:

A tree that India doth not yield,
    Nor ever yet was seen,
Where buds of virtue always spring,
    And all the year grow green.

That country's blest wherein she grows,
    And happy is that rock
From whence she springs: but happiest he
    That grafts in such a stock.

SINCE FIRST I SAW YOUR FACE

SINCE FIRST I saw your face I resolved
    To honour and renown you :
If now I be disdain'd, I wish
    My heart had never known you.
What, I that loved and you that liked,
    Shall we begin to wrangle?
No, no, no ! my heart is fast,
    And can not disentangle.

If I admire or praise you too much,
    That fault you may forgive me ;
Or if my hands had stray'd to touch,
    Then justly might you leave me.
I ask'd your leave, you bade me love :
    Is 't now a time to chide me?
No, no, no ! I 'll love you still,
    What fortune e'er betide me.

The sun, whose beams most glorious are,
    Rejecteth no beholder ;
And your sweet beauty, past compare,
    Makes my poor eyes the bolder.
Where beauty moves, and wit delights,
    And signs of kindness bind me,
There, O there, where'er I go,
    I leave my heart behind me.

If I have wrong'd you, tell me wherein,
    And I will soon amend it ;

In recompense of such a sin,
  Here is my heart ;— I 'll send it.
If that will not your mercy move,
  Then for my life I care not.
Then, O then, torment me still,
  And take my life, and spare not !

FROM CAMPION'S AIRS

THE RIGHT OF BEAUTY .

GIVE BEAUTY all her right,
  She 's not to one form tied ;
Each shape yields fair delight
  Where her perfections bide :
Helen, I grant, might pleasing be ;
And Rosamund was as sweet as she.

  Some the quick eye commends,
    Some swelling lips and red :
  Pale looks have many friends,
    Through sacred sweetness bred :
Meadows have flowers that pleasure move,
Though roses are the flowers of Love.

  Free Beauty is not bound
    To one unmovèd clime ;
  She visits every ground,
    And favours every time :
Let the old loves with mine compare,
My Sovereign is as sweet and fair.

THREE POOR MARINERS

WE be three Poor Mariners,
    Newly come from the seas :
We spend our lives in jeopardy
    While others live at ease :
Shall we go dance the round, the round, the round?
Shall we go dance the round, the round, the round?
    And he that is a bully boy
Come pledge me on this ground, aground, aground !

    We care not for those martial men
        That do our states disdain ;
    But we care for the merchant men,
        Who do our states maintain :
To them we dance this round, around, around,—
To them we dance this round, around, around,—
    And he that is a bully boy
Come pledge me on this ground, aground, aground !

FROM MELISMATA

THE THREE RAVENS

THERE were three Ravens sat on a tree,—
    Down-a-down, hey down, hey down !
There were three Ravens sat on a tree,—
                With a down !
There were three Ravens sat on a tree,—
They were as black as they might be :
With a down, derry derry derry down down !

The one of them said to his make —
Where shall we our breakfast take?

Down in yonder greenè field
There lies a knight slain under his shield.

His hounds they lie down at his feet:
So well they their master keep.

His hawks they fly so eagerly,
There's no fowl dare him come nigh.

Down there comes a fallow doe,
Great with young as she might go.

She lift up his bloody head,
And kist his wounds that were so red.

She gat him upon her back,
And carried him to earthen lake.

She buried him before the prime;
She was dead ere even-time.

God send every gentleman
Such hounds, such hawks, and such leman !
　　　　With a down, derry ——

FROM PILKINGTON'S MADRIGALS

HAVE I FOUND HER?　O rich finding !
　Goddess-like for to behold :
Her fair tresses seemly binding
　In a chain of pearl and gold.
Chain me, chain me, O Most Fair !
Chain me to thee with that hair.

PHILLIDA AND CORYDON

PHILLIDA — CORYDON ! arise, my Corydon !
    Titan shineth clear.
CORYDON — Who is it that calleth Corydon ?
    Who is it that I hear ?
PHILLIDA — Phillida, thy true love, calleth thee :
    Arise then, arise then,
    Arise and keep thy flock with me !
CORYDON — Phillida, my true love, is it she ?
    I come then, I come then,
    I come and keep my flock with thee.

PHILLIDA — Here are cherries ripe, my Corydon !
    Eat them for my sake !
CORYDON –- Here 's my oaten pipe, my Lovely One !
    Sport for thee to make.
PHILLIDA — Here are threads, my true love ! fine as silk,
    To knit thee, to knit thee
    A pair of stockings white as milk.
CORYDON — Here are reeds, my true love ! fine and neat,
    To make thee, to make thee
    A bonnet to withstand the heat.

PHILLIDA — I will gather flowers, my Corydon !
    To set in thy cap.
CORYDON — I will gather pears, my Lovely One !
    To put in thy lap.

PHILLIDA — I will buy my true love garters gay,
For Sundays, for Sundays,
To wear about his legs so tall.
CORYDON — I will buy my true love yellow say,
For Sundays, for Sundays,
To wear about her middle small.

PHILLIDA — When my Corydon sits on a hill,
Making melody,—
CORYDON — When my Lovely One goes to her wheel,
Singing cheerily,—
PHILLIDA — Sure, methinks, my true love doth excel
For sweetness, for sweetness,
Our Pan, that old Arcadian knight;
CORYDON — And methinks my true love bears the bell
For clearness, for clearness,
Beyond the Nymphs, that be so bright,

PHILLIDA — Had my Corydon, my Corydon,
Been, alack! her swain,—
CORYDON — Had my Lovely One, my Lovely One,
Been in Ida plain,—
PHILLIDA — Cynthia Endymion had refused,
Preferring, preferring
My Corydon to play withal.
CORYDON — The Queen of Love had been excused
Bequeathing, bequeathing
My Phillida the golden ball.

PHILLIDA — Yonder comes my mother, Corydon!
Whither shall I fly?

CORYDON — Under yonder beech, my Lovely One !
    While she passeth by.
PHILLIDA — Say to her thy true love was not here !
    Remember ! remember
To-morrow is another day !
CORYDON — Doubt me not, my true love ! do not fear !
    Farewell then ! farewell then !
Heaven keep our loves alway !

Ignoto.

BEAUTY SAT BATHING

BEAUTY sat bathing by a spring
    Where fairest shades did hide her :
The winds blew calm, the birds did sing,
    The cool streams ran beside her :
My wanton thoughts enticed mine eye,
    To see what was forbidden ;
But better memory said — Fie !
    So vain desire was chidden.
        Hey nonnie ! nonnie !

Into a slumber then I fell,
    When fond imagination
Seemed to see, but could not tell
    Her feature or her fashion.
But even as babes in dreams do smile,
    And sometimes fall a-weeping,
So I awaked, as wise this while
    As when I fell a-sleeping.
        Hey nonnie ! nonnie !

Shepherd Tonie.

WHERE HIS LADY KEEPS HER HEART

SWEET LOVE, mine only treasure !
   For service long unfeigned,
    Wherein I nought have gained,
Vouchsafe this little pleasure :
      To tell me in what part
      My Lady keeps her heart.

If in her hair so slender,
   Like golden nets entwinèd
    Which fire and art have finèd,
Her thrall my heart I render,
      For ever to abide
      With locks so dainty tied.

If in her eyes she bind it,
   Wherein that fire was framèd
    By which it was inflamèd,
I dare not look to find it :
      I only wish it sight
      To see that pleasant light.

But if her breast have deigned
   With kindness to receive it,
    I am content to leave it,
Though death thereby were gained.
      Then, Lady ! take your own,
      That lives for you alone.

                    A. W.

THE TOMB OF DEAD DESIRE

WHEN VENUS saw Desire must die —
     Whom high Disdain
     Had justly slain
For killing Truth with scornful eye,—
The earth she leaves, and gets her to the sky :
     Her golden hair she tears ;
     Black weeds of woe she wears ;
For help unto her Father doth she cry :
     Who bids her stay a space,
     And hope for better grace.

To save his life she hath no skill :
     Whom should she pray?
     What do, or say,
But weep for wanting of her will?
Meantime Desire hath ta'en his last farewell,
     And in a meadow fair,
     To which the Nymphs repair,
His breathless corse is laid with worms to dwell.
     So glory doth decay
     When Death takes life away.

When morning's star had chased the night,
     The Queen of Love
     Look'd from above,
To see the grave of her delight ;
And as with heedful eye she view'd the place,
     She spied a flower unknown,
     That on his grave was grown

Instead of learned verse his tomb to grace.
  If you the name require,
  Heart's-case, from dead desire.

A. W.

HOPELESS DESIRE
SOON WITHERS AND DIES

THOUGH naked trees seem dead to sight,
    When Winter wind doth keenly blow,
Yet, if the root maintain her right,
    The Spring their hidden life will show :
But if the root be dead and dry,
No marvel though the branches die.

While hope did live within my breast,
    No winter storm could kill desire ;
But now disdain hath hope oppress'd
    Dead is the root, dead is the spire.
Hope was the root, the spire was love :
No sap beneath, no life above.

And as we see the rootless stock
    Retain some sap, and spring awhile,
Yet quickly prove a lifeless block,
    Because the root doth life beguile,—
So lives desire which hope hath left :
As twilight shines when sun is reft.

A. W.

NATURAL COMPARISONS
WITH PERFECT LOVE

THE LOWEST trees have tops, the ant her gall,
The fly her spleen, the little sparks their heat ;
The slender hairs cast shadows, though but small ;
And bees have stings, although they be not great ;
Seas have their source, and so have shallow springs :
And love is love, in beggars as in kings.

When rivers smoothest run, deep are the fords ;
The dial stirs, yet none perceive it move ;
The firmest faith is in the fewest words ;
The turtles can not sing, and yet they love :
True hearts have eyes and ears, no tongues to speak ;
They hear and see and sigh, and then they break.

A. W.

IN PRAISE OF THE SUN

THE GOLDEN SUN that brings the day,
And lends men light to see withal,
In vain doth cast his beams away
Where they are blind on whom they fall :
There is no force in all his light
To give the mole a perfect sight.

But thou, my Sun ! more bright than he
That shines at noon in summer tide,
Hast given me light and power to see,
With perfect skill my sight to guide :
Till now I lived as blind as mole
That hides her head in earthly hole.

I heard the praise of Beauty's grace,
Yet deem'd it nought but poets' skill;
I gazed on many a lovely face,
Yet found I none to bind my will:
Which made me think that beauty bright
Was nothing else than red and white.

But now thy beams have clear'd my sight
I blush to think I was so blind;
Thy flaming eyes afford me light,
That beauty's blaze each where I find.
And yet these Dames that shine so bright
Are but the shadow of thy light.

A. W.

BEGGARS' SONG

BRIGHT shines the sun : play, beggars ! play !
Here 's scraps enough to serve to-day.

What noise of viols is so sweet
   As when our merry clappers ring?
What mirth doth want where beggars meet?
   A beggar's life is for a king :
Eat, drink, and play ; sleep when we list ;
Go where we will, so stocks be miss'd.
Bright shines the sun : play, beggars ! play !
Here 's scraps enough to serve to-day.

The world is ours, and ours alone,
   For we alone have worlds at will :
We purchase not, 'tis all our own,
   Both fields and streets we beggars fill.

Nor care to get, nor fear to keep,
Did ever break a beggar's sleep.
Bright shines the sun : play, beggars ! play !
Here 's scraps enough to serve to-day.

A hundred head of black and white
    Upon our gowns securely feed :
If any dares his master bite,
    He dies therefore, as sure as creed.
Thus beggars lord it as they please :
And only beggars live at ease.
Bright shines the sun : play, beggars ! play !
Here 's scraps enough to serve to-day.

IF WRONG BY FORCE

IF WRONG by force had Justice put to flight,
    Yet were there hope she might return again ;
If lawless War had shut her up from sight,
Yet lawful Peace might soon restore her train :
But now, alas ! what hope of hope is left,
When wrongful Death hath her of life bereft?

The Sun, that often falls, doth often rise ;
The Moon, that waneth, waxeth full with light :
But he that Death in chains of darkness ties,
Can never break the bands of lasting night.
What then remains but tears, of loss to wail
In which all hope of mortal help doth fail?

In vain I live, such sorrow lives in me ;
In vain lives Sorrow, since by her I live :

Life works in vain where Death will master be ;
Death strives in vain where Life doth virtue give.
Thus each of us would work another's woe,
And hurts himself in vain, and helps his foe.

Who then shall weep — nay, who shall tears refrain,
If common harms must move the minds of all?
Too few are found that wrongful hearts restrain,
And of too few too many Death doth call.
These common harms I wail among the rest,
But private loss denies to be express'd.

FROM WIT'S RECREATIONS

ON A BEAUTIFUL VIRGIN

IN THIS MARBLE buried lies
Beauty may enrich the skies,
And add light to Phœbus' eyes.

Sweeter than Aurora's air,
When she paints the lilies fair
And gilds cowslips with her hair.

Chaster than the virgin Spring,
Ere her blossoms she doth bring,
Or cause Philomel to sing.

If such goodness live 'mongst men,
Bring me it ! I shall know then
She is come from heaven agen.

But if not, ye standers by !
Cherish me, and say that I
Am the next design'd to die.

ON CHLORIS WALKING IN THE SNOW

I SAW FAIR CHLORIS walk alone
When feather'd rain came softly down, —
Then Jove descended from his Tower
To court her in a silver shower :
The wanton snow flew to her breast,
Like little birds into their nest ;
But overcome with whiteness there
For grief it thaw'd into a tear ;
Then, falling down her garment hem,
To deck her, froze into a gem.

ON HIS MISTRESS

MY LOVE and I for kisses play'd,
She would keep stakes, I was content,—
And when I won she would be paid :
This made me ask her what she meant.
Saith she - - Since you are in this wrangling vein,
Take you your kisses ; give me mine again !

PHILLADA

OH ! WHAT a pain is love :
    How shall I bear it?
She will unconstant prove,
    I greatly fear it.
She so torments my mind,
    That my strength faileth,
And wavers with the wind
    As a ship saileth :
Please her the best I may,
She loves still to gainsay :
Alack and well-a-day !
    Phillada flouts me.

All the fair yesterday
    She did pass by me,
She look'd another way,
    And would not spy me :
I woo'd her for to dine,
    But could not get her ;
Will had her to the wine —
    He might intreat her.
With Daniel she did dance,
On me she look'd askance :
Oh, thrice unhappy chance !
    Phillada flouts me.

Fair maid ! be not so coy,
    Do not disdain me !

I am my mother's joy :
    Sweet ! entertain me !
She 'll give me when she dies
    All that is fitting :
Her poultry, and her bees,
    And her goose sitting,
A pair of mattrass beds,
And a bag full of shreds :
And yet, for all this guedes,
    Phillada flouts me.

She hath a clout of mine,
    Wrought with blue coventry,
Which she keeps for a sign
    Of my fidelity :
But, 'faith, if she flinch,
    She shall not wear it ;
To Tib, my t' other wench,
    I mean to bear it.
And yet it grieves my heart
So soon from her to part :
Death strike me with his dart !
    Phillada flouts me.

Thou shalt eat crudded cream
    All the year lasting,
And drink the crystal stream
    Pleasant in tasting,
Whig and whey whilst thou lust,
    And ramble-berries,
Pie-lid and pastry crust,
    Pears, plums, and cherries ;

Thy raiment shall be thin,
Made of a weevil's skin ——
Yet all 's not worth a pin :
  Phillada flouts me.

Fair maiden ! have a care,
    And in time take me !
I can have those as fair,
    If you forsake me :
For Doll the dairy maid
    Laugh'd at me lately,
And wanton Winifred
    Favours me greatly.
One throws milk on my clothes,
T' other plays with my nose :
What wanting signs are those !
    Phillada flouts me.

I can not work nor sleep
    At all in season :
Love wounds my heart so deep,
    Without all reason.
I 'gin to pine away
    In my Love's shadow,
Like as a fat beast may
    Penn'd in a meadow.
I shall be dead, I fear,
Within this thousand year :
And all for that my dear
    Phillada flouts me.

NOTES

NOTES

DUNBAR

DUNBAR begins the sixteenth century: 1503 is the date of *The Thistle and the Rose*, written on occasion of the marriage of James IV of Scotland with the English Princess Margaret. *The Golden Targe* (printed at the first Scottish Press) was written somewhat later. The two poems I print are undated: probably one or both belonging to his younger days. How could these so simply beautiful lines on the Rue have escaped the collectors? Is there much so fine through all the poetic years? Not only to show what antique spelling was, I repeat them here, *verbatim et literatim*, from Laing's edition of Dunbar, 1834.

To a Ladye

Sweit Rois of vertew and of gentilness,
Delytsum Lyllie of everie lustyness,
  Richest in bontie, and in bewtie cleir,
  And everie vertew that is held most deir
Except onlie that ye ar mercyless.

Into your garthe this day I did persew,
Thair saw I flowris that fresche wer of hew;
  Baithe quhite and reid moist lusty wer to seyne,
  And halsum herbis upon stalkis grene;
Yit leif nor flour fynd could I nane of Rew.

I dout that Merche, with his cauld blastis keyne,
Has slane this gentill herbe, that I of mene :
   Quhois petewous deithe dois to my heart sic pane,
   That I wald mak to plant his rute againe
So comfortand his levis unto me bene.

Page 1, *line* 4 : — Pinkerton, who printed this in his *Ancient Scottish Poems*, 1786, has —

   And everie vertew the to hevin is deir.

Garthe is garden ; *I of mene* — I moan for, or lament ; *comfortand* (a termination often in old writings) — comforting ; *been* — were, or have been. This use of *been*, as also for *are* and *is* and *be*, is common in early poetry : —

   With every thing that pretty bin — Shakspere.
   Thy words harsh and ungracious been — Chapman.
   As fresh as been the flowers — Peele.

P. 2 — ADVICE TO LOVERS. *Leir* — learn; *perquier* — truly, says Laing, but it is the French *pourquoi*, Italian *perche*, — therefore, wherefore, reason why ; *is went* — is gone, of the verb *to wend* — to go ; *discure* — discover.

HEYWOOD

P. 3 — A PRAISE OF HIS LADY. Out of *Tottel's Miscellany*, 1557. Reprinted by Arber, 1870. Ellis in his *Early English Poets* has the poem wanting the seventh stanza. In the line

   She may be well compared,

I hope I may be forgiven for adding *very*, to help the halting measure : more likely the printer's than the poet's fault.

WYATT

P. 5 — YEA OR NAY. *Boordes, boords,* or *bourdes,* — tricks. jests. Here is a specimen of bad punctuation, from Ellis : —

   If it be yea, I shall be fain ;
    If it be nay — friends as before :
   You shall another man obtain ;
    And I, mine own ; and yours no more.

P. 6 — DISDAIN ME NOT !
> Forethink me not, to be unjust!

That is — Do not be unjust in thinking ill of me before cause
shown !   Arber has —
> Nor think me not to be unjust ;

And Ellis —
> For think me not to be unjust,

Both meaningless !   *Forethink* is used by Donne ; Chapman
has also *forespeak.*   And *foregone, forewent, forefeels.*
> But since ye know what I intend.

Since is here used for when, or after : the stanza is complete.
Ellis, with a comma in place of the full stop, alters the sense.
He also misprints the last line of the poem :
> Forsake me not now for no new.

VAUX

P. 7 — DEATH IN LIFE.   Given in *The Paradise of Dainty
Devices,* 1576 ; and Morley's *New Book of Tablature,* 1596.
Reprinted in Collier's *Lyrical Poems,* 1844.

TUSSER

P. 8 — This, from the *Hundred Good Points of Husbandry,*
is in the original entitled *A Sonnet ;* and may in some sort be
considered such, if we take it as consisting of fourteen verses,
the first twelve but divided into two lines each to expose the
middle rhymes.   The old printer in line 4 for *gift* had *shift,*
destroying sense and rhyme too ; in line 13 for *poor face* had
good face, also senseless.

GRIMAOLD

P. 9 — A TRUE LOVE.   The old reading of line 5 is —
> As mellow pears above the crabs esteemed be.

But surely the poet did not emphasize *the ;* and would mark
the contrast to *mellow* with some descriptive word, *harsh,* or
other : though I may not have hit upon the right.   In the last
line but one I dare to print *or* for *and.*

GOOGE

P. 11 — TO THE TUNE OF APELLES.

Her face of crystal to the same.

So in Arber's *Reprint* of his *Eglogs, Epitaphes & Sonettes,* Googe, 1563. Her *face,* or *eyes?* "Crystal eyes" was the stock poetic simile. Yet Watson has "her crystal breast."

P. 12 — ONCE MUSING AS I SAT. This appears at first like long lines arbitrarily divided, each second half (Arber's copy) beginning without a capital. But the division is at the accent, except in one instance, where a comma enforces it at the cost of sense: the well-rejoicing of the Fly being so altered to the well-perceiving of the man. *Sely* — simple, guileless. foolish.

SIDNEY

P. 17 — ABSENCE. In Ward's *English Poets,* 1880, part of this is given : one stanza squeamishly suppressed. I will not meet ill thought by pointing out which. Honi soit qui mal y pense! Pure and manly, there is never one word of Sidney's that needs to be blotted out. One may here also remark the unfairness, toward both writer and reader, of giving only part of a short poem. It should be all or none. Yet frequently in collections we find not even notice of omissions.

I offer no apology for giving so much from so true a poet, characterized at once (as Grosart well observes) by "passion, thought, and fineness of art," and so neglected : out of whose riches so late a collector as Trench can borrow only a couple of sonnets. Palgrave's *Golden Treasury,* a choice gathering, and assuming "to include in it ALL THE BEST original lyrical pieces and songs in our language," contains (notwithstanding the Laureate's "advice and assistance") TEN lines of Sidney, those incorrectly. The lovely *Epithalamium* (here at p. 22) will bear comparison with the *Epithalamion* and *Prothalamion* of Spenser, or with Ben Jonson's *Epithalamion* (p. 61). There is another Marriage Song of equal beauty by rare Ben :

" Glad Time is at his point arrived," to be read in his *Masque of Hymen*. And Donne has yet another of the same sterling character: "The sunbeams in the East are spread." Four of these neglected by the excellent collectors; and of Spenser's two one distinctly rejected by Palgrave, as " not in harmony with modern manners."

My first four Songs and first three Sonnets will be found in the *Astrophel and Stella;* the EPITHALAMIUM, EPITAPH, RURAL POESY, and the second Sonnet on p. 29, are from the *Arcadia*. It is of this last sonnet that Palgrave gives part as complete in two five-line stanzas. He perhaps followed Ellis, who found it in Puttenham's contemporaneous *Art of Poesy;* yet neither Ellis nor Palgrave is exact to Puttenham. And he may have trusted to memory, or to some musical miscellany where it had been altered to a song, to suit an air. With few differences of punctuation, Dr. Grosart's careful text warrants me here, and generally for Sidney's writing. The exceptions are noted as follows.

P. 16 — THE MEETING. In the last stanza he has —
> Leaving him to passion rent :

Pp. 17 – 18 — ABSENCE. —
> Or if I myself find not :
> Fearing her beames, take with thee

(which places the accent awkwardly on *her*) :
> O my thoughts, my thoughts surcease !

(But he himself observes that the poet addresses Thought as " his intellectual part," " a being that has thoughts,"—which also would require *thy* thoughts, as *thy* delights in next line)
> Till thou shalt ruinèd be,

(without comment,— surely a misprint) :

P. 21 — THE COLLOQUY.—
> More then in thy reason's sight:
> No, the more fooles it doth shake

(which is not the poet's sense, even if his own writing) :

P. 25 — EPITHALAMIUM.—
> But keeping whole your meane,

(What mean between peacock pride and sluttery? Or would Sidney have missed the regularly recurring rhyme?):

P. 26. — WOOING STUFF.—
> In question? nay, 'uds-foot, she loves thee than.

(*Than* — then. I leave out the useless *'uds-foot*, doubting it to be Sidney's, also as out of measure. Ellis rejects it.)

P. 30 — HIS ANSWER.—
> Deeming strange euill in that he did not know.

Fire and *sire* (in desire), p. 14, must be read as dissyllables, sometimes written *fier* and *desier*; *but* means unless, in last stanza of OPPORTUNITY; *destines* is destinies; *minds* (such minds to nourish, p. 21) is desires, thoughts, minded things; *louts* — obeisances, courtesies (p. 21); *grant to the thing* is grant the thing (p. 23); *learn* (p. 26) has its old meaning of teach: a *sleek-stone* (p. 27) is a stone used for smoothing, or sleeking, leather; *wood* (p. 30), also *wode*, is mad.

WATSON

P. 31 — ON SIDNEY'S DEATH. Taken from Byrd's *Italian Madrigals*, 1590. Collier, reprinting it in his *Lyrical Poems*, for *With dreary* has *How with dryry*; for *then*, in last line but one, *therefore*, spoiling the rhythm; and *greeting*, in the last line, to rhyme with *weeping*. Since in all Watson's verse I have detected but one false couplet, and that looking like a misprint, I will not believe that in eight lines on so serious an occasion he would have been content with such slovenliness. I only suggest *keeping*, as at least to the purpose. I doubt any dependence to be placed on early texts, more particularly referring now to musical miscellanies. I suspect that the old musical editors, Byrd, Campion, and the rest (supposed or known to have sometimes written upon their own account), cared very little, if at all, for verbal exactness, and would not hesitate to alter their poet's words to suit the music: a more

tolerable practice, I dare to think, than mangling our old airs
to fit new words,—as was done with Moore's Melodies. But
then we must disenthrone these editors as literary authorities.
Byrd, or Bird, or Byrde, or Birde, was Watson's associate in
the first publication of Madrigals with English words: that is
to say, "Italian Madrigals Englished, not to the sense of the
originall dittie, but after the affection of the noate." In which
collection are "excellent madrigalls of Master William Byrds,
composed after the Italian vaine at the request of the sayd
Thomas Watson."

Pp. 31–34 — These five "Sonnets" (so miscalled, consisting
all of six-lined stanzas) are from Watson's *Hekatompathia*,
or a "*Passionate Centurie of Loue*, diuided into two parts:
whereof the first expresseth the Author's sufferance in Loue:
the latter his long farewell to Loue and all his tyrannie." 1582.
THE MAY QUEEN is from *England's Helicon*. The Sonnet,
pp. 35 – 36, from *The Teares of Fancie, or Loue Disdained*,
" printed at London for William Barley. dwel*ling* in Gratious
streete, ouer against Leaden Hall, 1593." Put not your trust
in printers ! This one mis-spells the name of his own streete.
There was no *Gratious streete* in London ; but, named from
the church in it, Gracechurch St. — over against Leaden Hall.
Merest poetic conceits as Watson's verses seem to me, when
compared with the passionate, heart-welling poetry of Sidney
(though Arber, who not inaptly styles Watson " our English
Petrarch," would rank him above Sidney, next after Spenser),
they are worth notice, not only for their rarity, but also for a
display of very extensive book-learning, and more as perhaps
the best of a large proportion of the Euphuistic versification
of the period. Arber's *Reprint* of the *Tears of Fancy*, 1870,
is "from an unique copy" owned by S. Christie-Miller, Esq.

Each of Watson's hundred (97 only) Sonnets, or Passions,
has for prefix a prose annotation : a single example of which
may suffice to show the affected, yet learned, quality of all.

The following explains the sonnet I call THE KISS, p. 33:—

"In this passion the Authour, being ioyfull for a kisse, which he had receiued of his Loue, compareth the same vnto that kisse, which sometime Venus bestowed vpon Aesculapius, for hauing taken a Bramble out of her foote which pricked her through the hidden spitefull deceyte of Diana, by whom it was laide in her way, — as Strozza writeth. And hee enlargeth his inuention vppon the french prouerbiall speech, which importeth thus much in effect,— that three things proceed from the mouth, which are to be had in high account, Breath, Speech, and Kissing;—the first argueth a man's life; the second his thought; the third and last, his loue."

P. 31 — OF TIME. In Davison's *Poetical Rhapsody* this has been reduced to a sonnet, by throwing out four lines.

P. 32 — JEALOUS OF GANYMEDE. Arber prints in the first stanza, or "staff" —

To which all Neighbour, Saintes and Gods were calde.

In the third —

And she once found should neither will nor choose.

P. 35. — *Randon* is random; *blaze*, blazon. In Byrd's *Italian Madrigals* I find the following variation of the MAY QUEEN. Was it so changed to suit "the affection of the noate"?

TO THE MAY QUEEN

This sweet and merrie month of May,
While nature wantons in her pryme,
And byrds do sing and beasts do play,
For pleasure of the joyfull time;
I chuse the first for holly daie,
And greet Eliza with a ryme.
O beauteous queene of second Troy,
Take well in worth a simple toy.

I may here add, as farther sample of a poet almost unknown, a fragment (which as such would not come within the limits of my text) from his "MELIBOEUS, an Eglogue," translated by Watson from his own Latin Elegy written on the death of

Sir Francis Walsingham, 1590.   Spelling of Gratious streete.
Diana is of coursé Queen Elizabeth.

. . DIANA, wondrous mirrour of our daies ;
　　Diana, matchlesse Queene of *Arcadie;*
　Diana whose surpassing beauties praise
　　improus hir worth past terrene deitie ;
　Diana, Sibill for hir secret skill ;
　　Diana, pieties chief earthlie friend;
　Diana, holie both in deede and will ;
　　Diana, whose iust praises haue no end.
Ah but my Muse, that creeps but on the ground,
　　begins to tremble at my great presume,
For naming hir, whose titles onelie sound
　　doth glad the welkin with a sweet perfume.
For in hir minde so manie vertues dwell
　　as eurie moment breed new pieties :
Yet all in one coioind doe all excell,
　　and crowne hir worth with sundrie deities.
But that vnwares my sorie stile proceeds
　　drad *Cynthia* pardon : loue desires dispense :
As *Joves* high Oaks orelook *Pans* slender reeds,
　　so boue all praising flies thine excellence.
Yet lest my homespun verse obscure hir worth,
　　sweet *Spencer* let me leaue this taske to thee,
Whose neuerstooping quill can best set forth
　　such things of state, as passe my Muse, and me.
Thou *Spencer* art the alderliefest swaine,
　　or haply if that word be all to base,
Thou art *Apollo* whose sweet hunnie vaine
　　amongst the Muses hath a chiefest place.
Therefore in fulnes of thy duties loue,
　　calme thou the tempest of *Dianaes* brest,
Whilst shee for Meliboeus late remoue
　　afflicts hir mind with ouerlong vnrest.

MUNDAY

P. 36—The DIRGE out of an old play, *The Death of Robert Earl of Huntingdon*, the joint production of Henry Chettle and Anthony Munday: Munday's authorship of these lines is therefore not quite certain. The play is reprinted in the 1874 edition (W. C. Hazlitt's) of Dodsley's *Old Plays*.

PEELE

Pp. 37, 38 — These two songs are from *The Arraignment of Paris*, a "pastoral" performed before Q. Elizabeth in 1584.

GREENE

Pp. 39–45 — The Eclogue, MENAPHON'S ROUNDELAY and SONG, are out of his *Menaphon*, afterwards called *Arcadia;* INFIDA'S SONG from *Never too late;* SWEET CONTENT from his *Farewell to Folly*. Line 7 of DORON AND CARMELA is corrected by Dyce to —

> Thine eyes are like the glowworms:

but the whole Eclogue is burlesque, and not to be reconciled with common sense.

P. 41 — INFIDA'S SONG. The burden Englished thus : —

> Sweet Adon! darest not glance thine eye —
>> Will you not dare? my pretty friend!
> Upon thy Venus that must die?
> I pray you, let your scorn have end! (pity me!)
>> Will you not dare? my fair! my fair!
>> Will you not dare? my pretty friend!

I have accented *prië*, since it must be read as if two syllables (pri-e): the usual French poetic measure, used by Chaucer and other early English writers, probably the original of the later *a* at the end of a line, as in —

> Your sad heart tires in a mile-a.

P. 44 — SWEET CONTENT. Although since deciding on my selection, I find this in Ward's *English Poets*, latest and best of our anthologies, I retain it, because I think I detect errour in one line as there printed (as it is also printed by Dyce) : —

> The sweet consort of mirth and music's fare.

What is there peculiar to an obscure life in the consorting of mirth and music? And what may be *music's fare?* Mirth and *modest fare* are noticeable consorts, if *modest* be not the word Greene wrote. I think he did not write *music's;* while he might have left the second stanza in the unreadable shape his editors allow it to preserve, thus :—

> The homely house that harbours quiet rest ;
> The cottage that affords no pride nor care ;
> The mean that 'grees with country music best ;
> The sweet consort of mirth and music's fare ;
> Obscurèd life sets down a type of bliss :
> A mind content both crown and kingdom is.

> Ward's *English Poets* — vol. 1. p. 409.

A not unfair specimen this of the ease with which an author's meaning can be obscured by only wrong punctuation. Dyce prints these lines in an equally unsatisfactory manner, except that he alters *a type* to *as type*, so helping toward the sense ; while Ellis keeps the obscuring *a*, and destroys sense with a full stop after *fare*. I prefer *the mean agrees* (*that* understood — no unusual construction) to *the mean that 'grees*.

DRAYTON

Pp. 46 – 50 — WHAT LOVE IS, ROWLAND'S ROUNDELAY, and the SONG OF MOTTO AND PERKIN, are in his Eclogues. In my copy (edition 1619), p. 46, line 4, *ceaseth* is printed for *seizeth;* p. 49, line 14, *breath* is repeated. carelessness of poet or printer. *Make*, p. 47, line 3, means mate, often so used in old poems ; p. 50, *stervèd* is starvèd, *clip* is clasp.

DAVIES

Not Sir John Davies, but plain John Davies, writing-master, of Hereford, "the greatest Master of the Pen that England in her age beheld," says Fuller ; as a poet not without esteem of his great contemporaries, yet of whose existence I obtain no trace in the anthologies. Even Ward, 1880, has ignored him, though two quarto volumes of *Davies' Poetical Works* were

published in 1878, rescued from oblivion by the indefatigable
Dr. Grosart. To me, as to Dr. Grosart, " Wotton is thin and
feeble beside these finely woven lines "—his PICTURE OF AN
HAPPY MAN, "albeit *How happy is he born and taught* has
secured its place in our literature."   Davies' poem appears in
the *Rights of the Living and the Dead*, put as Appendix to
his *Muse's Sacrifice*, printed in 1612 ; Wotton's may be dated
at least two years later.

His principal works are *Microcosmos, Humours Heau'n on
Earth* (in which is a Dantesque *Picture of the Plague*, that
of 1603), *Witte's Pilgrimage, The Scourge of Folly* - for the
most part *satyrical epigrams*, and *The Muse's Sacrifice or
Divine Meditations*.

P. 51. line 11 —*squire* is old French *esquierre*, a carpenter's
square ; p. 52, line 14, *moe* or *mo* — more (old usage, held to
now in parts of America).

P. 54 — IN PRAISE OF MUSIC.   Davies' heading is —
  " To the Lady Wroth : in the deserved praise of heavenly
    musick, resembling it to God himselfe."

Am I too venturesome, altering Grosart's *joyful* to *joyless* in
            The lively death of joyful thoughts?

Lively — life-like, living.

P. 55 — AN HELLESPONT OF CREAM : by master Davies
thus prefaced :—
  — "The Author loving these homely meates specially viz.,
    Creame, pancakes, butterd pippin-pies (laugh good people)
    and tobacco; writ to that worthy and vertuous gentlewoman
    whom he calls mistrisse, as followeth."

NASH

P. 56 — FAIR SUMMER.   Sung in *Summer's Last Will and
Testament :* Dodsley's *Old Plays*.   Hazlitt (W. C.) gives in
the first stanza *Go not yet away*, and *Go not yet hence* in the
second.

MARKHAM

P. 57 — SIMPLES.   From a play by Markham and Sampson,

therefore given to Markham with some doubt. But Gervase, or (as he signs his name) Jervis Markham deserves especial remembrance for his "*Tragedy*" *of Sir Richard Grenville*, a full and particular account of that most daring of sea-fights, Grenville's action off Florez, in 1591 : written in 174 stanzas of eight lines, not without poetic merit, however overwrought and high-flown. A brief extract may show its form.

> When Grinuile saw his desperate drierie case ;
>
> . . . .
>
> Gallants (he saith) since three a clock last noone,
> Vntill this morning, fifteene houres by course.
> We haue maintaind stoute warre, and still vndoone
> Our foes assaults, and driue them to the worse.
> Fifteene *Armados* boardings haue not wonne
> Content or ease, but beene repeld by force,
>>   Eight hundred cannon shot against our side
>>   Haue not our harts in coward colours died.
>
> Not fifteene thousand men araungd in fight
> And fifteene howers lent them to atchiue.
> With fifty three great ships of boundlesse might
> Haue had no meanes or prowesse to contriue
> The fall of one, which mayden vertue dight
> Kept in despight of *Spanish* force aliue.
>>   Then list to mee you imps of memorie ;
>>   Borne to assume to immortalitie.

DONNE

Pp. 58 – 60 — Campbell chose the BREAK OF DAY, sufficient *imprimatur*, one would think, and assurance against neglect by later collectors ; Emerson disinterred the UNDERTAKING. its theme perhaps too exalted for general appreciation ; every one has missed the FUNERAL. Cramped as these songs are by Donne's quaint pedantry, they are true poetry. With all his faults, Donne stands above the crowd in our anthologies.

JONSON

Pp. 61 - 79 — The EPITHALAMION is the close of a Masque "on occasion of Lord Haddington's marriage at Court, on the Shrove Tuesday at night," 1608. IF I FREELY is in the play of *The Poetaster;* HER MAN, "described by her own dictamen," IN THE PERSON OF WOMANKIND — a song apologetic, BEGGING ANOTHER, and HIS EXCUSE FOR LOVING, are all from his collection of poems called *Underwoods,* the neglect of which is specially noticed, but is not revenged, by Trench. *In the person of Womankind* is given by Campbell. Note what a full Shaksperian flavour is in the SATYRS' SONG, from *Oberon!* What song but Ariel's will dare to match with it? HER GLOVE, sometimes called The Glove of the Dead Lady, is from the play of *Cynthia's Revels.* Here — lines 5, 6, Dyce follows the old reading — *wear thee, bare thee.* MARGARET RATCLIFFE makes an acrostic. The SONG OF NIGHT is in the *Vision of Delight,* a masque.

DAVISON

Pp. 71 - 76 — TO URANIA and her ANSWER are by Francis ; the other poems may be by either of the brothers. They are from Davison's *Poetical Rhapsody,* first printed in 1602, and containing poems by Raleigh, Watson, Sylvester, and others named, besides many anonymous pieces.

P. 71 — Sir Egerton Brydges, followed by Sir Harris Nicolas, in the last stanza, or staff, of the poem to URANIA has *their ire.* Ellis gives five stanzas of the poem, omitting the fourth, and calls it *Strephon's Palinode.*

P. 74 — UPON HER PROTESTING. Nicolas here adopts other readings : stanza 2, lines 2, 3, —

> Or face well-form'd and fair —
> Or long, heart-binding hair ;

stanza 3, line 3 —

> Or your enchanting grace.

BEAUMONT AND FLETCHER

P. 77 — TELL ME! is by Fletcher. Of this two versions are extant: that I have given, from the play of *The Captain*, and one in *The Knight of the Burning Pestle*. Instead of *'Tis a grave*, &c. in the first stanza, the copy there has :—

> SHE — 'Tis a smile
> Doth beguile
> HE — The poor hearts of men that prove.

And the second stanza also reads differently, as follows :—

> HE — Tell me more! Are women true?
> SHE — Some love change, and so do you.
> HE — Are they fair and never kind?
> SHE — Yes! when men turn with the wind.
> HE — Are they froward?
> SHE — Ever toward
> Those that love to love anew.

The third stanza is wanting. Here Dyce has *wise* for *wiser*.

P. 80 — HYMN TO PAN. Dyce (edition 1846) has —

> From that place the morn is broke :

which is ungrammatical nonsense. *Where morning broke*, I have no doubt, gives Fletcher's meaning, though these very words be not his. He certainly wrote fair English. Another and often quoted Song to Pan — "All ye woods and trees" is in the same most beautiful of all pastoral comedies, Fletcher's *Faithful Shepherdess*.

The other four Songs may probably be by Beaumont : the WEDDING SONG in *The Maid's Tragedy*, the DANCE SONG in *A Masque of the Middle Temple*.

BURTON

P. 81. This poem is prefixed to his *Anatomy of Melancholy*.

DRUMMOND

P. 85 — SEXTAIN. *Sith*, old usage, for since. The same in DEATH NOT FEARED, p. 86 ; and in the Madrigal at p. 246.

P. 87 — SWEET ROSE.   To rhyme with *kiss'd* in the last line
I have *bliss'd.* instead of *bless'd:* the same meaning.

P. 88 — A DÆDAL OF MY DEATH.   Turnbull's edition, 1856,
copying the Edinburgh edition of 1616, has —

> Now I resemble that subtle worm on earth
> Which, prone to its own evil, can take no rest:

two lines devoid of rhythm.   Rescuing the rhyme restores
the sense.   *Semble,* though out of use, is a good dictionary
word, as likely a word as *semblance* or *semblant,* used by
Spenser.   *Uneath* (rhyming with *death*) is uneasy, here taken
as restless: also Spenserian.   "The field is *eath* to win,"
Gascoigne writes; and Fairfax, in his *Tasso* —

> Who thinks him most secure is *eathiest* shamed.

Ill was, I think, more often used than *evil* by old writers.

FIELD

P. 88 — MATIN SONG.   All the copies have —

> And ignorance, darker than night.

WEBSTER

P. 89.   From that most noble nor less powerful tragedy,
The Duchess of Malfy.

BROWNE

P. 90.   From the Second Book of *Britannia's Pastorals.*

HERRICK

P. 91 — The *Hesperides* is so rich in jewelry, that the most
careless selection can hardly be unsatisfactory.   Yet being so
rich, there might have been more independent taste.   One is
led to ask how much of popular favouritism even in literature
is, like fashion in clothes, due to dictation of the purveyors.

P. 93 — PANSIES : *pensées* (French), thoughts.   "Pansies for
thoughts," says Ophelia.   Drayton gives our more commonly
used English name : —

> The pansy heart's ease maidens call.

BRATHWAITE

P. 96. Or Brathwait. "A noted wit and poet;" his writings "were numerous." So Ellis, giving two samples of his verse: this, which is also entitled *Care's Cure*, "from *Panedone, or Health from Helicon*, 1621;" and a fragment, of like quality, from his *Shepherd's Tales. Callet* is scold. In line 2 of the first stanza Ellis prints —

> Take the world as it is.

In line 3 of the fourth stanza he has *slop-wise* for *slope-wise.* And in line 3 of the fifth stanza —

> [Where] lesser flies are quickly ta'en.

GOFFE

P. 98 — To Sleep. Stoddard, in his choice but insufficiently known *Melodies and Madrigals*, 1866, has line 5 ---

> Morpheus, be kind a little and be.

SHIRLEY

P. 100 — Hue and Cry. From his Poems. In his play of *The Witty Fair One* I find another version, here subjoined.

> IN LOVE'S NAME you are charged hereby
> To make a speedy hue and cry
> After a face, who t' other day
> Came and stole my heart away.
> For your directions, in brief,
> These are best marks to know the thief.
> Her hair, a net of beams, would prove
> Strong enough to captive Jove,
> Playing the eagle; her clear brow
> Is a comely field of snow;
> A sparkling eye, so pure a grey
> As when it shines it needs no day;
> Ivory dwelleth on her nose;
> Lilies married to the rose
> Have made her cheek the nuptial bed;

Her lips betray their virgin red,
As they only blush'd for this,
That they one another kiss :
But observe ! beside the rest,
You shall know this felon best
By her tongue,— for if your ear
Shall once a heavenly music hear,
Such as neither gods nor men
But from that voice shall hear again,
That, that is She : O take her t' ye !
None can rock heaven asleep but she.

P. 102 — SONG TO HYMEN.   In line 6 Dyce prints *chafe* for *chase*.   Has *f* been mis-set for the old-fashioned long *ſ*, and escaped the printer's reader ?   *Chafe* does not seem right.

HABINGTON

P. 104 — QUI QUASI FLOS EGREDITUR (Who cometh up as a flower) : from the Third Part of *Castara :* a homily on the text — *Job*, 14, 2.   How beautifully turned into a compliment at the close !

P. 105 — FINE YOUNG FOLLY Campbell gives to Etheridge, but it is printed in Habington's *Queen of Arragon*, a " tragicomedie," published in 1640 ; the poet Etheridge was born in 1636.   If written by an Etheridge, it must have been an elder, under whom Richard Edwards, known as a " deviser of" and a contributor to *The Paradise of Dainty Devices*, is said to have studied music.   In the last line for *Bedlam* might we not rather read *Beldam* — belle dame ?

SUCKLING

P. 113 — A BALLAD OF A WEDDING.   I have found this in *Witt's Recreations*, a selection " from the Finest Fancies of Modern Muses " 1654, where (headed with a coarse wood-cut of two waggoners, as if it had been first published as a street

song) it appears as " a Discourse between two countrymen."
Hazlitt (W. C.) thinks it was addressed to Suckling's friend
Richard Lovelace. It may have been so: but the Dick of the
ballad is my fellow-waggoner. The "two countrymen" must
not be lost sight of. It is for that reason I retain those little
nice touches of rusticity,— *volk* and *vorty* for *folk* and *forty*,
Widson for *Whitsun*. They add a charm of true-semblance
which is lost in the exchange for politer verbiage. Indeed one
noticeable beauty of the ballad is the rare mixture of courtly
grace with country manners: the "countryman" not boorish,
and the courtier a true waggoner. *Hard by* (second stanza)
is the street still known as the Hay-market. *Course-a-park*
I take to be the name of some village dance or game.

The Ballad has been printed incorrectly in the first edition
of Suckling's Works, 1646; and the text is also corrupt in two
editions issued by Jacob Tonson, 1709, 1719: "God B' w' y'!"
(so printed in 1654 — *God be with ye!* confused with kisses)
becoming *Good Boy*. Ellis' copy agrees generally with mine;
though he too accepts the *Good Boy*. Against all versions I
venture to print *best* in line 3 of the third stanza for *rest:* the
bridegroom's place not being first in the procession, but first
of the best. He would hardly be spoken of as " amongst the
rest " and at the same time " before the rest." Perhaps also,
Suckling may have used a better rhyming *pace* in stanza 18:
the last line on p. 116.

The selectors seem to have been afraid of giving the whole
of this most delicious ballad, a ballad " of twenty-two incomparable verses, of wonderful brightness and sweetness," fairly
so described by Mr. Gosse in his excellent introduction of the
poet, in Ward's *English Poets*. Even there we have sixteen
only of the "incomparable verses," one as of old incorrect and
out of place : and what is yet worse, the fragment printed as
if whole, without notice of excision except the few words I
quote, not necessarily seen by readers of the Ballad. But the

omitted stanzas may (my readers can judge for themselves) be " not in harmony with modern manners," as Mr. Palgrave so prettily phraseth it, and as some Rev. Mr. Suckling would seem also to have imagined, who gives with a Memoir of the Poet only the usual sixteen stanzas, without note or apology. A fastidiousness scarcely honest while Shakspere, not yet out of harmony, is on every gentleman's table.

P. 119 — A HEALTH. I confess my own liability to reproach for altering this pearl of the wine-cup toward modern liking. The penultimate line in each stanza displaces one — the same in all three stanzas by Suckling : which a poetical reader will easily restore.

P. 120 — BARLEY-BREAK needs explanation. It was a game played by six persons, three of each sex, coupled by lot. The play-ground was divided into three, the middle part was Hell. The couple first condemned, holding hands, tried to catch the other couples running across the middle ground, the pursued being allowed to separate if too hard pressed. Jamieson. in his *Etymological Dictionary,* speaks of the game, played in Scotland with a dule, or goal, in a stack-yard.

> At barley-break her sweet swift foot to try

says Sidney, describing the game in a long poem in *Arcadia.* Among Morley's *Madrigals* also we find one upon it.

> LOVE'S FOLK in green arraying
> At barley-break were playing:
> Laura in Hell was caught ;
> Then, O how Dorus laught,
> And said — Good Mistress ! sith you
> Will thither, needs have with you !

Notice here the rhyming of *caught* and *laught !*

RUTTER

Pp. 122 – 3. Two Songs from *The Shepherds' Holiday,* for which see Dodsley's *Old Plays,* W. C. Hazlitt's edition, 1875.

Virginhed—virginity. So in Spenser is found *maidenhed* for maidenhood, *drowsyhed* for drowsiness, &c.

CRASHAW

P. 124—WISHES. Another of the always mutilated poems: the length of this perhaps sometimes an excuse. Ward omits twenty-six of the forty-two triplets; but, except in two cases, honestly marks where the omissions occur. Palgrave, besides arbitrarily transposing stanzas, omits twenty-one, not pointing where: content with informing us that he has "attempted to bring it within the limits of lyrical unity!" So others.

My copy is from the third edition of Crashaw's *Delights of the Muses*, 1670; but compared with Dr. Grosart's *Complete Works of Crashaw*, 1872. I find in both:—

> Meet you her, my wishes,

(a syllable too much for the measure):

> Which to no boxe his being owes:
> Blushes that bin

(rhyming to the eye as well as to the ear):

> Vertue their mistresse,

(from which, I judge, a word has been dropped):

> 'Bove all, nothing within that lowers

(the modern spelling, *lours*, more exact to the meaning):

> Whose merit dare apply it.

LOVELACE

P. 129— THE GRASSHOPPER. The Chiswick reprint (1818), which I followed in my *Golden Apples of Hesperus*, for *ear*, in the first line, has *hair*, perhaps to better suit the *beard* in the second. I have since thought that Lovelace would write *ear:* though no more correct botanically, as the oat does not grow like wheat in ears, but in spikelets.

A strange piece of criticism on this poem, stranger from so accomplished a critic as Mr. Gosse, prefaces the eight stanzas given in Ward. Mr. Gosse writes what follows.

"In the curious verses entitled The Grasshopper, of which we shall presently give all that is intelligible, we seem to possess an instance of his hurried and jejune mode of composition. He commences by addressing the grasshopper, in lines of unusual dignity and pregnancy, but he presently forgets this, and without sign of transition, recommences 'Thou best of men and friends,' this time plainly addressing the friend, Charles Cotton, to whom the ode was sent. It is difficult to believe that he ever himself read over his lines, for it could not fail to occur to him, had he done so, that the same object could not be spoken to as 'Poor verdant fool' and as 'Thou best of men and friends.'"

Ward's *English Poets:* vol. 2, p. 183.

The same object is not so spoken to. Having described the brief summer joys of the grasshopper, poor verdant fool, now only green ice, and pointed the moral for us, to "lay in 'gainst winter," he turns naturally to his friend Cotton. Thou best of men and friends! he says, *we* will not be content with such grasshopper joys ; *we* " will create a genuine summer in each other's breast. and, spite of this cold time, our sacred hearths shall burn eternally." Whereupon most appropriately follows the other omitted as " unintelligible " stanza —

Dropping December shall come weeping in :

his ice-crown melting off at the cheerful fireside warmth, but reconciled and recrowned, a king again, with the brightness of their classic talk. How could Mr. Gosse, himself a poet, miss so obvious an understanding ? Did he not remember the

Sidneian showers
Of sweet discourse, whose powers
Can crown old Winter's head with flowers?

P. 130. Ward, not using a capital to *Vestal* (stanza 7) loses its full meaning : not only virgin flames, but the never-extinguished fire in Vesta's temple. In the next line the omission of a comma gives us the absurd image of a *dissolving Ætna*. Are these small things ? They show how easily texts can be obscured. They indicate perhaps that commas and capitals, whether of printer or editor, can not always be depended on.

MARVELL

P. 136 — CLORINDA AND DAMON.   In line 8 *vade*, from the
Latin *vadere*, to depart; "useful in poetry, but not received,"
says Dr. Johnson.   Used by Shakspere, as distinct from *fade*.
Brathwaite again marks the difference :—

> Thy form 's divine, no fading vading flower.

P. 138.   Our Pan's *quire:* old spelling for choir, as *quirister*
for chorister.   Dear quirister! writes Drummond.

BROME

P. 142 -- BEGGARS' SONG.   *Remore* — hinder: a word I can
not find in another author ; nor in the dictionaries.   It is from
the Latin, *Remora*, the name of a fish supposed "to stick to
ships and retard their progress."   Milton makes it English :

> The sum is, they thought to limit or take away
> the remora of his negative voice.

Richard Brome was the author of fifteen plays : his brother,
Alexander, of one.

VAUGHAN

·*P*. 143 — EPITHALAMIUM.   From "*Olor Iscanus*, a collection
of select poems and translations by Henry Vaughan, Silurist,
published by a friend, 1651."   Ellis gives three broken stanzas,
apologizing for their "too much quaintness and conceit."

The second stanza in my copy has *he* and *his*.   I hesitated
before altering this (for all the strangeness of a he Rose and a
she Sun), for the author may have so written.   The pronouns
are often confused in these old texts.

HALL

P. 147 — EPITAPH.   From Poems of John Hall of Durham.
1646, reprinted at Longman's Private Press, 1846.

FLETCHER

P. 148.   Of whom I find nothing except the date of 1656 to a
small volume of Translations from Martial, Epigrams, &c.

FLECKNOE

P. 149. Who had some poetic gift, notwithstanding Dryden. CHLORIS is in a little book, containing also his "*Diarium* or Journal, divided into 12 Jornadas, in burlesque rhyme or drolling verse," 1656.

BULTEEL

P. 150. Ritson speaks of him as secretary to Clarendon. He was the author of one play, *Amorous Oruntus*, or *The Love in fashion*. Campbell gives a song by him. The one I give should perhaps have had place among the poems by authors unknown, coming in "a collection written by several persons, never printed before" (156 pp.), lettered on the back and also written inside — "by John Bultiel." 1674.

TOTTEL'S MISCELLANY

The first edition of this earliest of collections has for all title:

SONGS AND SONETTES
written by the ryght honorable Lorde
Henry Howard late Earl of Sur-
rey, and other.
Apud Richardum Tottel, 1557. *Cum privilegio.*

This first edition, published June 5, contains 36 poems by Surrey, 90 by Wyatt, 40 by Grimaold ; and 95 by "uncertain authors,"— of which last two are attributable to Vaux, one to Heywood (that I have printed at p. 3), and one to Somerset. The second edition, July 31 in this same year 1557, contains 39 additional poems by anonymous writers. My selection is mainly from the first 95, only the last three from those added. The book was reprinted, carefully edited by Arber, in 1870.

Pp. 153-4 — THE MEAN ESTATE HAPPIEST. Arber has —
> Rule is enmy to quietness.
> That quite nights he had more slept.

P. 155 — LOVE'S DISDAINER. The second and fourth lines of the third stanza give *saught* and *laught* as rhymes; in the fifth stanza are *caught* and *laught;* and in the last *caught* and *taught.* Was *laught* pronounced hard?

P. 158 — PROMISE OF A CONSTANT LOVER. *Tene* — grief, grievous trouble; *let* — hindrance. In place of *let* Arber has *thret:* but he has also *thrette* in the second line. I but guess it should be *let.* However, the poet himself may be in fault. Spenser has the identical duplication: in canto XI, stanza 21, of *The Legend of Holiness :*—

> When wintry storm his wrathful wreck does threat
> — Then 'gin the blustering brethren boldly threat.

And canto VI, stanza 36, *new* with *knew,* and *red* with *red :*

> That in his armour bare a croslet red —
> To tell the sad sight which mine eies have red.

Let it be confessed that all our difficulties are not chargeable to the printer.

P. 160 — OF THE CHOICE OF A WIFE. In Tottel —

> Gives first the cause why men to heare delight,
> And yet not so content, they wish to see.

That, in third line of third stanza, is used for *what.*

Pp. 161 – 2 — OTHERS PREFERRED. In Tottel —

> The worse I speed the longer I watch.
> Since my will is at others lust.
> That helpeth them, lo! cruelty doth me kill.

In the first edition of Tottel this is attributed to Wyatt; in the second placed among the uncertain. Is this the only one too hastily attributed? Were these collecting publishers worthy of much trust? Was it all fish in their nets?

P. 162 — NO JOY HAVE I. *Relesse* is release; *lesse,* loss.

P. 163 — OF THE GOLDEN MEAN. *Guie* may be guide: *ne* is nor; *wonnes* — inhabits; *ruing* — perhaps only a misprint for rising; *one self Jove* — one same, one self-same Jove; *by course* — in turn; *'suage* — assuage (elision not infrequent).

P. 164 — THE PRAISE OF A TRUE FRIEND. *Reave* — reive, bereave: *eke* — also. These last three pieces come together in the Miscellany, and seem to be by one hand. I had hardly thought them worth giving but for the construction of verse.

THE PARADISE OF DAINTY DEVICES,

first appeared in 1576, purporting to be "devised and written for the most part by M. Edwards, sometime of her Majestie's Chappel ; the rest by sundry learned gentlemen both of honour and worshippe." Richard Edwards died in 1566. Was it the clever publisher's device? — this putting his name, he, as Ellis tells us, " being much esteemed for the variety of his talents, at once the best fiddler, mimic, and sonneteer, of the Court." An able composer also of church music and madrigals. His name very taking on a title-page. But "written for the most part." There are 100 poems in the first edition: only *eleven* of which are attributed to Edwards. In the edition of 1580 is an Appendix with 25 more, *two* by Edwards. In 1576 ten of the poems have *M. Edwards* subscribed ; one (at our p. 168) has *M. Edwardes May* superscribed. In the Appendix, four years later, there is a *Reply to M. Edwards May;* and in the same a rejoinder to that (surely not by Edwards, then dead fourteen years), *Maister Edwards his I may not.* Finding no other testimony, the doubtful look of this leads me to class " M. Edwards' " writings with those of authors uncertain.

P. 168 — MAY. In the *British Bibliography* of Brydges and Hazlewood this is printed in three stanzas of six lines each.

P. 165 — LIFE'S STAY. All but the first two lines in Dana's *Household Book of Poetry.* He mis-dates it 17th century.

BYRD'S SONGS

P. 169 — RIGHT CAREFULNESS. This is generally given to Byrd; but I can find no authority to justify the gift.

William Byrd, born about 1545, was a musician. Till 1588, says Oliphant in his *Musa Madrigalesca,* he seems "to have confined himself to the composition of sacred songs, motets, &c. *to Latin words;* but when about that time an importation of lighter strains arrived from Italy, he found it advisable to follow the new fashion." Byrd himself calls his first collection of Psalms and Sonnets the "first printed work of mine in English," meaning, I suppose, his first music with English words. The words *Out of M. Birds Set Songs*, in *England's Helicon*, I think, only imply that he wrote the music. These Set Songs I take to be his *Songs of sundrie natures*, 47 in all, "some of gravitie and others of mirth, fit for all companies and voyces, lately made and composed into musick of three, four, five and six parts, and published for the delight of all such as take pleasure in the exercise of that art. Imprinted at London by Thomas Este, the Assigne of William Byrd, 1589." There is nothing to affirm a claim as poet.

P. 171 — LOVE'S ARROWS. In Collier's *Lyrical Poems* —
There careless thoughts are freed of that flame.

P. 172 — THE HERD-MAN'S HAPPY LIFE. Ellis has —
And fortune's favours scorning.

In *England's Helicon* it is —
And Fortune's fate not fearing.

Presumptuous and *sumptuous*, with the different sounds of *s*, rhyme well, p. 173. Ellis does not give this stanza.

P. 175 — BROWN IS MY LOVE and CYNTHIA are from Byrd's *Musica Transalpina:* free translations probably. CYNTHIA, writes Oliphant, "is quite unintelligible and sets all the rules of common sense at defiance." He may well think so, with a semicolon ending the second line. Yet I conceive there is no lack of either sense or grammatical correctness. Cynthia! of Syrens the most commended, for that thou neither killest nor woundest, thy song awaketh in gentle hearts —— Surely he is a dull reader who can not understand this. The music may require *wanton Love maketh;* but *Love wanton maketh* had been better reading. Oliphant quotes it to praise the music.

THE PHŒNIX NEST

" Built up with the most rare and refined works of Noblemen,
Worthy Knights, Gallant Gentlemen, Masters of Arts, and
brave schollers,— full of varietie, excellent monition, and sin-
gular delight: never before published.   Set forth by R. S. of
the Inner Temple, Gentleman, 1593." The first poem in it is
Roydon's noble elegy on Sidney.   Peele, Watson, Lodge, and
others, were contributors.   Reprinted in Park's *Heliconia*.

P. 176 — THE ANATOMY OF LOVE.   In the *Phœnix Nest* it
is *A Description of Love:* my title is that given in Davison's
Poetical Rhapsody, 1602.   It is anonymous in both: though
ascribed to Raleigh in a *MS*. list of Davison's.   In *England's
Helicon*, 1600, it had appeared, the signature obliterated, as
The Shepherd's Description of Love: in a dialogue between
Melibœus and Faustus: beginning —

> Shepherd! what's love? I pray thee tell.

But the occasional shepherd is the chief difference.   Hannah
gives for the last line —

> And shepherd! this is love, I trow.

While Nicolas has it —

> And this is some sweet friend, I trow.

Sain is said.   The *sauncing*, sacring, or saints' bell is a small
bell used in the Romish Church to call attention to the more
solemn parts of the service of the Mass, as at the conclusion
when the priest repeats the words Sancte sancte sancte, Deus
Sabaoth!   Also at the elevation of the Host.

P. 177 — TO NIGHT.   In Park's *Heliconia*. 1815, *pleasures*
ends both first and third lines.   Campbell, in his *Specimens*,
1841, has *pleasure* and *treasure* :—

> There's none but only thou can guide me to my treasure :

contradicting the later line —

> Let them that miss the way be guided by thy light!

The second stanza Campbell omits.   Both he and Park have

> Hold in thy horns for shining.

DOWLAND'S SONG BOOKS

John Dowland, Bachelor in Musick and Lutenist to the King of Denmark, born about 1562, published between 1596 and 1603 three Books of Songs, Airs in four parts with tableture for the lute.

P. 179 — THE LOVER'S DESPAIR. *Flowers of spine* — thorn flowers. So in Fletcher —

> Roses, their sharp spines being gone.

Collier in his *Lyrical Poems* prints —

> Alas like flowers of Spain
> Thy graces rorie be:

with a note, suggesting *spine* for *Spain :* seeing "no reason why flowers of Spain should be more *dewy* than those of other countries." But, are flowers of spine more dewy than others? And what are dewy graces? He took *rorie* for granted : and it will be found in the dictionaries, "from the Latin *ros roris*, the dew." As authority, Webster cites Fairfax :—

> And shook his wings with rory may-dews wet.

Dewy dews? The dew on the pink-edged May-bloom would be rosy. *Rorie*, or *rory*, looks like a misprint in each of the above instances. Are there any more ? Did the dictionary-maker, dropping on the word, discover an etymology to suit?

P. 181, *l.* 2 — LOVE AND SORROW. Collier would here alter *hurt* to *heart ;* but the context shows *hurt* to be right.

P. 181 — SERENADE. In *England's Helicon* also, "taken out of Maister John Dowland's Tableture for the Lute."

P. 183 — TO CYNTHIA. Also in the *Helicon*, from Dowland, with "the Author's name not there set downe." On support of a copy "signed *W. S.*" having been found at Hamburg. in an English common-place book, it has been supposed that it was written by Shakspere. It has rather the trick of Raleigh, and is more worthy of him than most of the poems called his. *R*, the second stroke faint or defaced, might be taken for *S*.

P. 184 — WEEP YOU NO MORE! And whose this loveliest of songs? Worth especial notice is the beautiful close of each stanza (too easily spoiled by wrong punctuation) —

> That now lies sleeping softly,
> Now softly lies,
> Sleeping.

P. 185 — WHITE AS LILIES. *Quiting*, requiting. Collier has

> Quitting faith with foul disgrace.
> Careless of my bitter groaning,
> From her scant neglect proceeding.
> Should reward their friends as foemen.

And for the last line, wanting in the original, suggests —

> First to love, then leave forlorn.

But there is no first-loving in the song.

P. 187 — EYES AND HEARTS. Collier has —

> Makes our fraile pleasures eternall and in sweetness prove;
> Are still with sorrow declining unto deep annoies.
> If all one soul must love,
> By faith and merit united, can not remove;
> Distracted spirits
> Ten thousand beauties, yet in us one should be.

Surely, if dependence upon old texts can give us such results, we had better discharge our Dryasdust, be he printer's reader or editor, and trust the likelihood of common sense: it seems not altogether lacking in these early writers, in even the most careless of them. How pertinent here Collier's own remark: " Literal errors in the words to songs have been frequent from the earliest to the latest times;" and " woeful blunders transmitted to us in many of the productions of the poets."

P. 189   THE HERMIT'S SONG.   Two lines close each stanza: " conveyed" by Dowland from a song in Sidney's *Arcadia*.

> O sweet woods   the delight of solitariness:
> O how much do I love your solitariness!

Clearly they do not belong to the subject nor accord with the " sad groves" and " place of mourning;" but may have been appropriated to fit a lively change in the music? May we not regard it as a sample of the liberties taken by our musicians?

Wanstead House, near London, was a seat of the Earl of Leicester. Here Sidney wrote his masque, *The Lady of the May*, on occasion of a visit of Queen Elizabeth, in 1578. Was Raleigh retired there during some season of her displeasure? There is a look of him about this song, not unlike the lines to Cynthia; and what mistress but Majesty should appoint his place of retirement?

> Wanstead! my Mistress saith this is the doom.

"The mention of Wanstead," writes Collier, "shows that the piece, whatever it might be, whether play, masque, or other entertainment of a dramatic kind, was performed there." But the lines give no indication of their being part of anything.

P. 190 — LOVE AND FORTUNE. I place this with the Songs from Dowland's Books, first finding it there; a more correct copy appears (quite out of place) in Newman's 4to edition of Sidney. Collier reprints both: the Dowland version in 1844, in his *Lyrical Poems;* and the Newman version in 1865, in a note, in his *Bibliographical Catalogue of early English Literature*, introducing it with these words — "We are not sure whether the sprightly lines here imputed to the Earl of Oxford have ever been reprinted in modern times." Dowland omits the second stanza, and gives the third as here follows.

> Fortune sweares weakest harts,
> The booke of Cupid's darts,
>   Turne with hir wheele.
> Sences sometimes shall prove,
> Venture hir place in love,
>   Aske them that feele.

[Collier's *Lyrical Poems*, printed for the Percy Society, p. 82; *Bibl. Cat.*, vol. I, pp. 45–6.]

Venter — the belly. Fortune is speaking sneeringly. She may mean that mere condition of body is sometimes occasion of love, irrespective of any diviner incitement. Such seems to be also the sense in Dowland: but both the texts are obscure, and both most probably corrupt.

P. 194 — THE PEDLAR'S SONG. Collier, following Dowland, has *pinnes points, laces and gloves.* I think the pedlar was selling, not pins' points, but pins and points. A *point*, in my time even, in country places, was the name of a small tool for making holes in cloth, linen, &c., "eyes" for hooks to catch in.

MADRIGALS

P. 195. DEFIANCE TO LOVE is suspected to be by Drayton. I so gave it among my *Golden Apples.* Not finding it in his collected works, I place it here under the Uncertain Authors. MY DAINTY DARLING and other words with Morley's music may be his also. Morley was the first Englishman to produce a " Book of Balletts " (mistaken by Collier to mean Ballads). *Ballets* were songs set to music to be danced to. *Fear* is old usage for frighten, as in Shakspere —

For Warwick was a bug that fear'd us all.

P. 196 — FALSE CLARINDA. *Relying*, or leaning ; *persèver*, an old form of persevere. Very unsatisfactory the text (I do not attempt to mend it) of the second stanza, a stanza not in the *Helicon* copy.

P. 197 — FALSE DORUS. In *England's Helicon* as " Lycoris the nymph, her sad song." In last line of DAPHNE *fire* is a dissyllable, as in Sidney. Oliphant praises John Wilbye as the best of the madrigal composers.

P. 198 — THE JEWEL. Surely this is fragmentary : odd lines chosen for the air. Probably many of our old madrigals are no more : what suited the composer, or altered to suit.

P. 199 — LOVE ME NOT FOR COMELY GRACE. Ellis has it — *Love not me.* In line 8 I have *well* for *still.* Our poets were not scant of words, and even unmusical copyists are careless.

P. 201 — HOLD OUT, MY HEART! At first thought a rhyme seems wanted to *fie;* but I would rather conclude that it was wilfully omitted by the author. Only transposing *say* and *cry* would give the rhyme; but is not the ear better satisfied with the recurring sounds within the lines? *His full rewarding, i.e.* his love's. Weelkes was organist of Chichester Cathedral.

P. 205 — A MISTRESS DESCRIBED appears to be founded on, and more than the thought borrowed from, Heywood, p. 3.

P. 206 — SINCE FIRST I SAW YOUR FACE. Of this the first and third stanzas are often sung as a " Madrigal," but Hullah (who gives the fourth in brackets, as if doubtful) writing of such music says — " The vocal compositions of John Dowland, often incorrectly called madrigals, are for the most part songs with accompaniment for the Lute, or for three other voices. Though a contemporary of the great English madrigal writers, Dowland was not one of them. His compositions, like those of Forde, belong rather to the school of which, in England, Henry Lawes (Milton's friend) was the most accomplished master." [Notes to Hullah's *Song Book,* pp. 354 – 5.]

Excellent the music, and yet more note-worthy the perfect accord of words and music, of this, the choicest of madrigals or songs. I would fain believe that Forde wrote both, though there is only the internal evidence of its likelihood.

P. 207 — THE RIGHT OF BEAUTY. Words, as well as music, of this and other pieces have always been given to Campion, on the ground of their appearing as his in Davison's *Poetical Rhapsody.* Campion, says Ellis, was a physician, and also, adds Nicolas, famous for musical and poetical talent. And he is spoken of in connection with Watson as a good Latin poet. Two Books of Airs were composed by him. Four poems are set down as his in the *Rhapsody.* Probably these composers (he likeliest) did sometimes write words for their own music, but what really belongs to them as poets remains uncertain.

P. 208 — DEUTEROMELIA is the first, PAMMELIA the second, and MELISMATA the third, in a series of " Pleasant Rounde-lays, Delightful Catches, Freemen's Songs," &c., put forth by Thomas Ravenscroft. Was our THREE POOR MARINERS the original, or an imitation, of the better known song in the same collection ?—

> We be Soldiers three :
> Pardona moy, je vous an pree !
> Lately come forth of the Low Countrie,
> With never a penny of money.

Pp. 208 – 9 — THE THREE RAVENS. Words and music, says Chappell, as early as Henry the eighth. In the *Twa Corbies*, a Scottish version of this (which is the elder ?), copied from Ritson in Scott's *Border Minstrelsy*, hound, hawk, and lover forsake the dead knight. Is *earthen lake* the grave ; or is it Spenser's " lethe " or " limbo lake," which is under the earth ? *Leman* is lady-love. The burthen, or refrain, *With a down*, &c., follows every two lines.

ENGLAND'S HELICON

Or *The Muses' Harmony :* the first edition in 1600 with 150, the second in 1614 with 159 pieces, by the best Elizabethan poets : the richest and most varied of all the early collections. Here are the poems signed *Ignoto*, too hastily supposed to be by Raleigh. I have already taken of its contents.

P. 210 — PHILLIDA AND CORYDON. In the *Helicon* entitled *Phillida's Love-call to her Corydon and his Replying. Say*, in French *saie*, is a thin kind of serge.

P. 212 — BEAUTY SAT BATHING. *To Colin Clout* in *Helicon; Shepherd Tonie* is guessed to be Anthony Munday.

DAVISON'S POETICAL RHAPSODY

Pp. 213 – 17 — A. W. has baulked all inquirers. Not meaning disrespect to any, one can hardly refrain from observing that *A. W.* might hide *Anonymous Writer*. The first edition of the *Rhapsody* appeared in 1602 ; it was enlarged in 1608, and again in 1611 ; and re-arranged in 1621. Reprinted in 1814, at Lee Priory, by Sir Egerton Brydges. See Davison, p. 240.

P. 218 — IF WRONG BY FORCE. In Sir Harris Nicolas' reprint in 1826, he remarks that in the third edition a stanza omitted from the earlier editions had been added to *The Anatomy of Love*. Plainly not belonging to that, he removes it to a note. Further consideration would have shown him that, it is part (misplaced, I think, in making up the pages) of the following poem — IF WRONG BY FORCE. I give it as the third stanza.

Pp. 219, 20 — ON A BEAUTIFUL VIRGIN. Trench omits the last triplet ; and calls it *A Pagan Epitaph*. *Agen* — again.

P. 221 — PHILLADA. Author and date not known : but the air is referred to as "a new tune" in *The Crown Garland of Roses*, 1612. In Walton's *Complete Angler* we find —

Milkwoman! what song was it? I pray. Was it "Come, Shepherds! deck your heads!" or "As at noon Dulcina rested," or "Phillada flouts me," or "Chevy Chase," or "Johnny Armstrong," or "Troy Town"?

My version mainly adheres to Ellis, who refers to a poetical miscellany, *Wit Restored*, published in 1658. Ritson copies from another miscellany, *The Theatre of Compliments*, 1689. The two versions differ materially. My and Ellis' stanzas 4 and 6 stand in Ritson as 8 and 7, Ritson inserting another, I think spurious, as 4, between Ellis' 3 and 4 : as follows.

I often heard her say
 That she loved posies :
In the last month of May
 I gave her roses.
Cowslips and gillyflowers
 And the sweet lily
I got to deck the bowers
 Of my dear Philly.

> She did them all disdain,
> And threw them back again :
> Therefore 'tis flat and plain
> Phillida flouts me.

Besides this addition, I note the following as most important differences in the two versions. Ellis' copy seems to have a more original flavour; Ritson's to be more corrupt, yet sometimes correcting Ellis. In our stanza 2 Ritson has —

> Dick had her to the Vine.

No! *Will had her* with him (so Ellis) all the dinner through, *to the wine,* when the men were left to themselves.

Stanza 4 Ritson gives as under.

> But if she frowns on me,
>   She ne'er shall wear it;
> I 'll give it my maid Joan,
>   And she shall tear it.
> Since 'twill no better be,
>   I 'll bear it patiently;
> Yet all the world may see
>   Phillida flouts me.

Stanza 7. Ritson again —

> Which way soe'er I go,
>   She still torments me;
> And whatsoe'er I do,
>   Nothing contents me;
> I fade and pine away,
>   With grief and sorrow;
> I fall quite to decay
>   Like any shadow.

Here Ellis (*Wit Restored* — the earlier copy) reads —

> I 'gin to pine away
>   With grief and sorrow,
> Like to a fatted beast
>   Penn'd in a meadow.

Neither reading can be right, the alternate rhymes elsewhere regularly maintained. I correct with diffidence.

Stanza 3: *guedes* (*goods* in both Ritson and Ellis) — things. See Glossary to Scott's *Sir Tristrem.* Look also in Littré's

French Dictionary. Stanza 4: *clout*—a kerchief; *coventry*, some fabric made at Coventry, or perhaps a kind of thread for embroidery. The *blue* is Ritson; Ellis has *good*. In stanza 5 I venture on *crudded* (clouted or clotted) *cream* against both Ritson and Ellis, who have *curds and cream*. *Whig* is sour buttermilk, something between pure milk and whey: whence the name of the English Whig politician, as being neither one thing nor the other, like the Bat in the Fable. Drayton has —

> With green cheese, clouted cream, with flawns and custards
> stored,
> Whig, cider, and with whey, I domineer a lord.

And Warner in his *Albion's England*—

> Of whig and whey we have good store.

I may not leave unnoticed one line in Ritson, surely corrupt:

> Swigg whey till thou burst,

which Ellis but partly mends with —

> Whig and whey whilst thou burst.

Ramble-berry (Ellis) looks like the original of bramble-berry, the blackberry. In this same stanza Ritson has —

> Thin as a weather's skin,

And Ellis —

> Thin as a weaver's skin.

Wether might go for *weather*, if a sheepskin could be called thin. For *weaver*, unless weavers too are exceptionally thin-skinned, I would read *weevil*, a small delicate wheat-eating caterpillar (not the weevil beetle). In stanza 6 Ritson has—

> What pretty toys are those!

Ellis alters this to —

> What wanton signs are those!

In stanza 7 Ellis reads --

> And all for very fear!

Ritson —

> And all because my dear.

After all I can but make patch-work. The texts are evidently very corrupt, perhaps written from memory; and emendation is little more than guessing. Not four hundred years old is this song, popular, and not unappreciated by collectors, who had no interest in altering it,—one would think the very tune must help to preserve a correct form : and yet we can not be sure of the words ; and of the author there is not a trace.

I may conclude by adding to the list of poetical-and-musical publications, of the high song-time of England, *Fantasies in three parts*, composed for viols; and *Madrigals and Motets;* both by Orlando Gibbons. The last contains poems by Dyer, Sylvester, and others, mostly fragmentary : as, indeed, it may be repeated, many of the madrigal poems very probably are, even some of the few I have given.

Truly it was a music-loving age, and with verse and music right worthy of its love !

www.ingramcontent.com/pod-product-compliance
Lightning Source LLC
Chambersburg PA
CBHW030341270326
41926CB00009B/918